Houston

COMPARATIVE AMERICAN CITIES

A series edited by Joe T. Darden

Houston

Growth and Decline in a Sunbelt Boomtown

Beth Anne Shelton
Nestor P. Rodriguez
Joe R. Feagin
Robert D. Bullard
Robert D. Thomas

Temple University Press · **Philadelphia**

Temple University Press, Philadelphia 19122

Copyright © 1989 by Temple University.

All rights reserved

Published 1989

Printed in the United States of America

∞ The paper used in this publication meets the minimum
requirements of American National Standard for Information
Sciences—Permanence of Paper for Printed Library Materials,
ANSI Z39.48-1984

Library of Congress Cataloging-in-Publication Data

Houston : growth and decline in a sunbelt boomtown.

(Comparative American cities)
Bibliography: p.
Includes index.
1. Houston (Tex.)—Social conditions.   2. Houston
(Tex.)—Economic conditions.   3. Houston (Tex.)—
Ethnic relations.   I. Shelton, Beth Anne.   II. Series.
HN80.H8H7   1989   306'.09764'1411   88-29607
ISBN 0-87722-607-5 (alk. paper)

Contents

Acknowledgments   vii

Preface   ix

Series Preface   xi

1   Introduction: A Case Study of Houston, Texas   3

2   Economic Growth and Decline in Houston: 1836–1986   9

3   City and Suburban Politics: Changing Patterns of Political Determination   29

4   Neighborhood Groups and Development: A Question of Participation and Elites   55

5   Patterns of Racial and Ethnic Disparity and Conflict: The Black Community   70

6   Patterns of Racial and Ethnic Disparity and Conflict: Hispanic Communities   93

7   The Future of the City   123

Notes   137

Index   151

Acknowledgments

Few works in the academic community are products solely of their authors. This book is no exception. We are grateful to a variety of people and institutions who contributed their support in the shaping of this book. Our editor, Janet Francendese, shepherded the project skillfully through numerous permutations. Colleagues at our various institutions who read earlier drafts and deserve special thanks are Ben Agger, Arnoldo DeLeon, and William Norris. Hannah Blake provided helpful research assistance. We also are especially grateful to Joe Darden, Dean of the Urban Affairs Program at Michigan State University, whose vision of the Comparative American Cities Series was the basis for this book's production.

Research assistance was provided by Oberlin College, The University of Houston, and L. Alex Swan, Dean of the College of Arts and Sciences, Texas Southern University.

Preface

This book is one in a set of urban volumes originally envisioned by Professor Joe Darden, Dean of Urban Studies at Michigan State University. His innovative plan was to commission a series of analyses of the largest cities in the United States. Remarkably, there are few books on U.S. cities that cover a range of basic urban topics. Darden's vision was to remedy that situation.

Each of the books in the Comparative American Cities series is organized around a basic outline that includes attention to minorities, redevelopment policies, and intrametropolitan government relations, among other things. Our book on Houston, however, requires us to approach these issues in a different way, since Houston is quite different from the other cities in the series. Houston experienced unprecedented growth in the 1970s only to suffer from the unplanned nature of the growth and a downturn of the economy in the 1980s. For all the discussion of Sunbelt cities in recent decades, we have remarkably few systematic, book-length treatments of particular Sunbelt cities. It is our intention to take a step in the direction of addressing this serious omission in the Sunbelt literature with this volume on Houston.

Houston is an intriguing city, one whose dramatic growth was ignored by the nation's mass media until the late 1970s, when it suddenly became the center of much favorable journalistic attention. When the oil recession hit Houston in the mid-1980s, however, this journalistic preoccupation with prosperity in the "Golden Buckle of the Sunbelt" turned to negative assessments of the city's future, soon to be followed by much less media attention to the city. Fewer positive articles were being written by 1985–1987. This book attempts to go beyond superficial treatments of Houston to look at its historical context, its demographic features, its politics, its minority communities, and its economic characteristics from the early twentieth century to the present.

SERIES PREFACE

The Comparative American Cities series grew out of a need for more comparative scholarly works on America's urban areas in the post–World War II era. American cities are storehouses of potential assets and liabilities for their residents and for society as a whole. It is important that scholars examine the nation's metropolitan areas to assess trends that may affect economic and political decision-making in the future.

The books have a contemporary approach, with the post–World War II period providing historical antecedents for current concerns. Each book generally addresses the same issues, although the peculiarities of the local environments necessarily shape each account. The major areas of concern include uneven regional development, white middle-class suburbanization, residential segregation of races and classes, and central-city issues such as economic disinvestment, black political power, and the concentration of blacks, Hispanics, and the poor. Each city in the series is viewed within the context of its metropolitan area as a whole. Taken together, these studies describe the spatial redistribution of wealth within the metropolises—the economic decline of central cities and the economic rise of the suburbs—a redistribution facilitated by the massive construction of interstate highways in the 1950s, 1960s, and 1970s.

Since World War II the metropolitan areas included in this series have been increasingly affected by uneven economic and social development and by conflict between cities and suburbs and between the white majority and the growing nonwhite minority. The central cities of each metropolitan area have also been losing jobs to the suburbs. There has been a tendency toward growing income inequality between cities and suburbs and between blacks and whites. Economic growth and decline have followed closely the racial composition of neighborhoods—that is, black neighborhoods have declined, while white neighborhoods have generally grown.

All of these studies assess the ways central-city governments have responded to these issues. In recent years most central-city elected officials have attempted to provide services and employment opportunities on a more equitable basis and to implement a more balanced and progressive economic development agenda. Most central-city mayors have been elected with the strong support of minorities, and the mayors have often cooperated with the business elite in attempts to stimulate more economic

growth and to save the cities from further economic decline. Since this decline is related to structural changes in the economy within the context of uneven development, however, attempts at preventing the flow of jobs to the suburbs have largely failed, and the economic and social gap continues to widen.

There are no quick solutions to the economic, racial, and political problems of the cities in these studies. Though high-technology industries may play a part in each city's future, it is unlikely that they will produce as many jobs as are needed, or reduce the racial differences in unemployment rates. Blacks and other minorities who have limited spatial access to the areas of high-tech industries may not receive a fair share of their benefits.

Each city's plight is deeply rooted in America's problems of free-market economic investment, racial prejudice and discrimination, and the outmoded political structure that continues to separate the city from the suburbs, one suburb from another, the rich from the poor, and blacks from whites. As long as this structure remains, there is a strong probability that the situation will worsen, as population mobility continues to reinforce patterns of economic, social, and racial inequality, contributing to more racial and class conflict.

The problems of urban America require the immediate attention of government officials and the citizenry of this nation. New solutions involving changes in the political structure are long overdue. Our hope is that comparative studies such as these might provide the impetus for informed decisions and policies that will address the underlying problems besetting America's major urban areas.

Joe T. Darden, Series Editor
Comparative American Cities

Houston

1

Introduction:

A Case Study of Houston, Texas

Metropolitan Houston has been described as the largest boomtown, space city, oil capital USA, and capital of the Sunbelt in national newspapers and newsmagazines. For more than a century Houston has generated strong and dramatic images in the minds of observers. Some images of Houston have been intentionally sold to an unsuspecting public. Others have emerged out of outsiders' and insiders' perceptions, both accurate and distorted, of Houston's dramatic growth. Indeed, in the 1830s the city was sold aggressively to outsiders by the real estate developers who packaged the mosquito-infested swampland and called it Houston. They advertised what they saw as the potential city's virtues, particularly its business opportunities. Later, *Fortune* magazine called it the city that the depression missed.[1]

In the 1970s the mass media again discovered Houston, with numerous articles on southern growth appearing in *Time*, *Newsweek*, and *U.S. News and World Report*. Most stories could have been written by the chamber of commerce. In the mid-1970s a *Houston Post* columnist characterized Houston as a "better mousetrap sort of town."[2] The excitement of the space program has also been used to glorify the city: "Houston, the first word from the moon, is the last word in American cities. Big, strong, young, insufferably confident, Houston is rushing hellbent into tomorrow without much thought about the day after."[3] Observers have emphasized the booming newness of Houston; one architect has commented that "there is really no sense of history felt in the city. So everything is bright and shiny and new."[4]

In the late 1970s *U.S. News and World Report* commented on Houston's dynamic growth in typical fashion: "This is not a city. It's a phenomenon —an explosive, churning, roaring urban juggernaut that's shattering tradition as it expands outward and upward with an energy that stuns even its residents."[5] For decades popular and real estate journals have touted Houston's booming real estate market for investors. Corporations specializing

in industrial location counseling raved about Houston's "good business climate" as hundreds of local newspaper articles in northern towns and cities heralded Houston's economy to troubled northerners. In the 1970s national attention was generated by the capital flowing to Houston from other regions of the country, a capital flow expressed in the physical form of new economic and urban development. Industrial capitalists, finance capitalists, and development capitalists are the driving forces behind this city, which for many decades expanded both horizontally and vertically, currently sprawling over more than 1,000 square miles of the Texas Gulf Coast.

In contrast to Houston's image as a problem-free city, there were pockets of unemployment and poverty even in the boom years of the mid-1970s. Many of the poor are minorities. Over 81 percent of Houston's blacks lived in predominantly segregated neighborhoods in 1980. The situation is similar for Hispanics. Over 45 percent of Houston's population is black or Hispanic, but blacks, Hispanics, and whites are clustered in different sectors of the city, reflecting class lines as well as racial and ethnic divisions.

The mid-1980s brought a "bust" to this premier boomtown when the price of oil dropped dramatically. Layoffs of workers in oil-related industries in Houston exceeded 150,000 in the 1983 and 1986 recessions, and the official unemployment rate topped 13 percent. In addition, devaluation of the Mexican peso reduced the number of affluent Mexicans coming to the city to shop. The rising dollar made Texas' export items, including agricultural and manufactured products, much more expensive for foreigners, causing a drop in exports. Moreover, when the dollar's value declined in 1986, Texas' exports did not recover to the former level. Since much of these exports move through the Port of Houston, that part of the city's economy also suffered greatly. As a result of these multiple economic difficulties, northern newspapers began to report that the Sunbelt they had formerly celebrated was suffering a major decline. This book, then, is about Houston in times of growth and in times of decline.

In this chapter we seek to provide a backdrop against which the current situation in Houston can be evaluated, and to introduce the diverse nature of the city and its residents. Houston is indeed a city with a variety of communities, and to a large extent this book will focus on these various communities rather than on the city as a single entity.

Houston: The Early Decades

In 1836 Augustus and John Allen bought several thousand acres of land for a little over a dollar an acre and marketed the land to outsiders, including eastern settlers unfamiliar with the area which was marshy, mosquito infested, humid, and hot in the summer. An 1836 advertisement placed by the Allens in a Texas newspaper put it this way:

> The town of Houston is located at the point on the river which must ever command the trade of the largest and richest portion of Texas. . . . [it] will warrant the employment of at least *One Million Dollars* of capital, and when the rich lands of this country shall be settled, a trade will flow to it, making it, beyond all doubt, the great interior commercial emporium of Texas.[6]

The advertisement went on to extol the virtues of the new town—its accessibility by river, its potential as a government center, and its attractiveness as a railroad center. There was also an element of exaggeration about its climate:

> There is no place in Texas more healthy, having an abundance of excellent spring water, and enjoying the sea breeze in all its freshness.[7]

These land developers offered the land to commercial capitalists and ordinary settlers with the hope that Houston would become the regional center of commercial capitalism and of the government of the new Texas Republic.

Efforts to market Houston have been made by the local growth coalition from the early 1900s to the present. One early Houston advertisement declared that Houston's "city hall is a *business* house. She has no wards, no ward politicians, no graft." [8] At about the same time, Houston's superintendent of public schools wrote an article praising the school board as composed of "a high type of business man," further noting that Houston's success was the "result of business methods applied to public affairs." [9]

Prior to the oil boom in the first decades of the twentieth century Houston was a major commercial and shipping center. As a center for the sale and export of timber and cotton, Houston was also a major railroad hub. By the 1850s Houston had numerous railroad lines linking it to rural areas. By 1901 Houston was tied into major intercontinental railroads, linking the city to New Orleans and San Francisco. In 1900 nearly one-third of

all Houston wages and salaries paid in manufacturing went to Houstonians working for the railroads.[10] The regional headquarters of the Southern Pacific Railroad was in Houston. Railroad capitalists from the East and Midwest invested in other industries in the Gulf Coast area and promoted such investments to outside investors.

By the last decades of the nineteenth century Houston had become a major regional center for trade in lumber, cotton, and grains. The counties around Houston produced huge quantities of cotton. By the early decades of the twentieth century Houston had 12 cotton warehouses, six cottonseed-oil mills, seven cotton compresses, and a major cotton exchange. Between 1890 and 1930 Houston was a major cotton center and the home of Anderson-Clayton, for a time one of the largest cotton brokerage companies. Even before oil, Houston's size and concentration of financial, transportation, and commercial resources made it the economic gateway of the region.[11] It was in the 1890–1920 period that Houston became a major commercial marketing center.

Diversity

Houston has long been composed of a variety of distinct communities and neighborhoods. In this book we refer to this diversity of communities rather than to Houston as a single entity because Houston can only be understood in terms of its varied communities. Houston's diversity can be characterized in various ways. It is a city of ethnic and racial groups with large black and Hispanic communities. In addition, it has a growing Asian community. Houston's population is located in distinctive neighborhoods, each with its own characteristics and needs. Representing the variety of neighborhoods are hundreds of neighborhood associations.

Unlike some cities in which the major cleavage is urban/suburban, in Houston there are myriad divisions based on ethnicity, race, socioeconomic status, and neighborhood. Thus, when examining the nature of the city's growth, redevelopment, and government, we examine their effects on a variety of communities rather than on a uniform—or unified—Houston.

The Focus of the Book

For the average citizen the city of Houston as a larger sociological entity is barely noticeable. Neither its past nor its overall form is easily grasped.

For the tourist Houston is a place with hotels and entertainment centers such as Astroworld or the Johnson Space Center. For the historian it is Houston's past, not its driving present, that is of greatest interest. For sociologists the city is all these things and more. It is a set of urban patterns, a puzzle whose fundamental themes must be probed. Few in-depth portraits of cities have been written by social scientists. This is true for U.S. as well as foreign cities. Indeed, perhaps the most thorough study of a city by a social scientist prior to the 1980s was Janet Abu-Lughod's study of Cairo, Egypt. Writing more than a decade ago, Abu-Lughod noted that Cairo is "a city with pressing problems of land use, chaos, and inefficiencies, of human and vehicular congestion, of social disorder and poverty, striving vigorously to create a utopia." [12] Oddly enough, one could say exactly the same thing about Houston, half a globe away, in the 1980s. Beneath the chaos of Cairo, Abu-Lughod found orderly patterns in its development and underlying structure. In the analysis of Houston that follows, we also find orderly patterns and structure underlying its seemingly chaotic development.

An Overview of the Book

Chapter 2 discusses Houston's patterns of economic growth and decline since 1900, with an emphasis on the emergence of the oil industry in the 1920s. The flow of investment to Houston since that period has dramatically altered the physical face of the city, from the downtown office towers to the concentration of oil refineries and petrochemical plants on the east side of the city. This chapter also explores the way in which developments in the oil industry such as the increasing concentration of oil capital and the government intervention of the 1930s have shaped Houston's growth.

Chapter 3 examines the political history and structure of Houston and notes a number of basic political shifts and alignments in the course of Houston's development as a modern city. Attention is given to the myth of self-sufficiency and the role of the federal government in creating political structures. Additional focus is on the relationship between city and sub-urbs and the unique proliferation of municipal utility districts in Houston's extraterritorial jurisdiction (ETJ). Political alignments and coalitions are explored in three periods—grass-roots federalism, selected-advocacy federalism, and regulatory federalism. Internal political alignments are examined in the context of the changing relationship of the local government to state and national governments.

Chapter 4 looks at the historical antecedents of development in Houston and then examines how the processes of privately directed development affected most city neighborhoods. Within that context the chapter examines the activities of a variety of citizens' organizations that have attempted to grapple with the many problems associated with rapid growth and development in a free enterprise setting. Additionally, the responses of several business organizations to the recent economic decline in the city are addressed along with the impact of various community groups on development. Conflict between business and community groups is given substantial attention in a concluding section.

Chapter 5 examines the geographical distribution and neighborhoods of black Houstonians against the backdrop of Houston's economic growth and more than a century of racial discrimination. Particular attention is given to the emergence of black neighborhoods in the core city and to the long-term crisis of private and public housing there. Black suburbanization is seen to be modest. Issues of income, educational, and job inequality are explored in detail. A concluding section notes the conflict between blacks and whites over city services. The chapter demonstrates throughout that the basic relationship between black and white Houstonians has long been one of racial conflict and pervasive inequality. Since the days of slavery Houston's blacks have had to struggle to gain even a small place in Houston's prosperity.

Chapter 6 provides a similar portrait for Houston's most rapidly growing minority—Hispanic Americans—by studying the historical background, demography, and geographical distribution of the Hispanic population. The issue of undocumented immigrants from Mexico and Central America is addressed after a review of employment, occupation, and income disparities. The implication of this chapter is that Houston's immigration stream must be understood within a world context. Examples are presented of the persistent ethnic conflict between Hispanic and non-Hispanic Houstonians.

Chapter 7 examines some of the trends and problems facing the city of Houston, with particular emphasis on the decline in the oil and petrochemical industries and on the many social costs of rapid urban growth and decline.

2

Economic Growth and Decline
in Houston:
1836–1986[1]

Houston has been cited as the leading example of rapid city development since World War II, and its boom times and glamour have received considerable popular attention. Its currently severe economic problems, precipitated by the mid-1980s oil recession, have roots not in the 1960s or 1970s but in the 1920s, when this already large regional city more than doubled its population. Since 1850 Houston's rate of population growth per decade has averaged 66 percent, a level unparalleled over such a long period among American cities. Even in the Great Depression Houston continued to grow rapidly and was described by *Fortune* magazine as the "city that never knew the Depression." Coupled with the rapid population growth in the 1960–1980 period was an extraordinary building boom, reflected in the hundreds of new office towers, dozens of massive shopping centers, and numerous suburban developments.

This growth centered on one major industry, since Houston's complex economy was built on the production, marketing, processing, and distribution of raw materials—specifically, oil and gas. Houston's ties to the oil industry mean that local developments can be understood only within a national and world context. Its emergence as a metropolis is linked to private-sector and governmental decisions to emphasize automobile, truck, and diesel-locomotive transportation over mass transit. The expansion of Ford and General Motors in Detroit in the early twentieth century ensured that a major city—Houston—would develop near the new Gulf Coast and East Texas oil fields.

Houston's Growth and Development

The population data in Table 2.1 reveal that in every decade since 1850 metropolitan Houston's population has grown by at least one-fifth, a rate

Table 2.1   Metropolitan Houston's population growth: 1850–1990

Year	Total population	Numerical growth during decade	Percent increase
1850	18,632	16,809	
1860	35,441	13,545	38.2
1870	48,986	22,330	45.6
1880	71,316	14,908	20.9
1890	86,224	48,376	56.1
1900	134,600	51,154	37.9
1910	185,654	86,821	46.8
1920	272,475	204,095	74.9
1930	456,570	190,299	41.7
1940	646,869	300,631	46.5
1950	947,500	482,894	51
1960	1,430,394	568,922	39.8
1970	1,999,316	906,034	45.3
1980	2,905,350	1,040,050	35.7
1990	3,945,400		

Source: U.S. Bureau of the Census; Houston Chamber of Commerce, "Houston Data Sketch," 1981. Metropolitan data prior to 1950, growth data for the 1980s, and data for 1990 are estimates.

that is high even in comparison with cities in the more densely populated North during the same period. Between 1890, when the city's population was only 27,500 (86,224 in the metropolitan area) and it was ranked as the 112th-largest U.S. city, and 1980 Houston had become the fifth-largest U.S. city. By 1983 it was the fourth-largest. Natural increase, migration, and annexation contributed to this growth. The most rapid growth in the city's history came in the years 1920–1930. Absolute gains in metropolitan population have been half a million or more for the last three decades, with nearly a million added in the 1970–1980 period. In spite of this history of rapid growth, projections of a population of 4 million by 1990 now seem unlikely, as the mid-1980s economy has almost halted in-migration.

Major Periods of Houston's Development

Houston's history of development can be loosely divided into four major periods during which the city was transformed from an agriculture-based economy to one in which state-assisted corporate development was dominant.

The Era of Commercial Capitalism (1840–1901)

As indicated in Chapter 1, Houston began in the 1830s as a speculative real estate venture in a Gulf Coast swamp by two northern capitalists. In the next few decades Houston emerged as a city dominated by a healthy commerce in agricultural products. Lumber, grain, and cotton were commodities that generated an important infrastructure of railroads, warehouses, cotton gins, and banks servicing the Texas agricultural economy. At an early stage Houston was home for large cotton brokerage companies. As a result of its agricultural commerce base, by 1901 Houston had become a major railroad center in the area west of New Orleans, and it was the site of the regional headquarters of the Southern Pacific Railroad. By the end of this period Houston had grown to 44,000 people; including the surrounding counties the Houston area now exceeded 130,000 in population, although much of this population was rural.[2]

The Era of Competitive-Industrial
Capitalism (1901–1915)

The discovery of oil 90 miles east of Houston and subsequent discoveries closer to the city laid the foundation for Houston to become a major oil and gas city. In 1905 the Humble field near Houston began producing oil; by 1919 it was joined by two other major fields. Three-quarters of Gulf Coast oil came from these fields. Beaumont, although closer to many oil fields, did not have the railroad and banking services already developed in Houston, an important agricultural commerce center.[3] Contrary to growth-pole theories that see Sunbelt cities as bypassed until recently by economic growth, Houston's early economic dominance as an agricultural center laid the foundation for its subsequent dominance as an oil center.

Not long after the discovery of oil, several oil companies organized production in the new fields located in the greater Houston area. The new Texas Company came to Houston in 1908, in 1916 the Gulf Company, newly born in the Houston area oil fields, moved to Houston. In this early period Houston's local growth coalition played an important role in decisions about where to locate oil companies. Working together, local bankers, real estate investors, and other business leaders pressed for state subsidies to improve Houston's deficient port facilities in the 1902–1914 period. In 1910 effective lobbying by this growth coalition paid off in a $1.25 million grant to deepen the Houston ship channel, the largest federal grant to a local government up to that time (cf. Chapter 3 for details). The

improved port facilities were an important factor in attracting oil-related companies to the Houston area.

The Era of Oligopoly Capitalism (1916–1931)

By 1916 the larger oil corporations were beginning to dominate many sectors of the Texas oil industry; over the next decade they consolidated their shared control. Events that transpired in an industrial city a thousand miles from Houston encouraged rapid oil development by the major oil companies and helped transform Houston into an oil capital. Houston was thus linked to Detroit. The events taking place in Detroit in the decade prior to Houston's growth boom were greatly shaped by the mass production of the automobile.

Automobile production began in earnest in the 1908–1925 period; before that crude oil had been used primarily for kerosene, fuel oil, and lubricants. In 1914 there were 1.8 million cars and trucks registered in the United States, but just a decade later the number had grown by ten times to 18 million vehicles. As a result, motor fuel usage increased from 2.7 billion gallons in 1919 to 15.7 billion gallons in 1930.[4] There was also an increased demand from expanding industries for fuel oil and lubricants. In the first decades of the twentieth century oil was beginning to replace coal as the fuel of choice for locomotives and industrial plants. The need for raw materials loomed large during this period. In the 1916–1929 period, numerous oil refineries and other oil-related industrial facilities were built in the area in order to be near critical raw materials and reduce transportation costs. Houston's improving port facilities were attractive to the oil industry. The new job opportunities in oil-related plants and offices attracted workers from rural and small-town Texas, as well as from contiguous states.

The expanding demand for fuel oil and lubricants provided both the capital and an incentive for oil company executives to invest in Houston-area facilities. From 1920 onward, this Gulf Coast oil economy was well integrated into the national economy. The long-distance relationship with Detroit was not one of filtering or diffusion, nor did it reflect unplanned or random development. Rather, Detroit and Houston industries were functionally integrated, with Houston providing raw materials for automobile production. Corporate executives in the auto-truck and oil industries planned the investment strategies that decided the fate of these two linked cities.

In addition, key corporate investment decisions made outside Houston and Detroit molded the Houston economy. Corporate executives of major

oil companies and allied bank executives—mostly in the New York area —made the decisions about putting capital to work in the oil industry. In the case of the Texas oil industry, the number of these critical decision makers was declining as the oil industry became more concentrated and centralized. By 1930 nearly three-quarters of Texas oil production was in the hands of 20 companies, although there were some 14,000 crude oil companies in the United States at the time.[5] Major oil companies expanded horizontally by buying up other oil companies and moving into new oil fields and ventures, driving smaller companies out of business; they expanded vertically by buying up or adding on an array of subsidiaries dealing with aspects of the oil business from research to oil production and marketing. The headquarters of the major oil companies were mostly in northern (especially East Coast) cities. By the early 1920s even Texas-born companies like Texaco were being run primarily from their northern headquarters.[6]

Weakened by the trust-busting of 1911, Standard Oil pressed to increase its power in the Texas fields. In 1918 Standard Oil bought into a Houston company, the Humble Oil and Refining Company. The linkages between Eastern capital, the major oil companies, and Houston's growth as an oil center can be seen clearly in an examination of the economic trajectory of the Humble Oil and Refining Company, which was formed by local Texas oilmen in 1917. These Texas entrepreneurs merged the resources of several small companies; they needed capital. Loans from local banks were at first utilized, but soon Humble Oil sought out New York banks for sizeable loans.[7]

Humble Oil's independence, and its capital problems, did not last long. In 1919 Standard Oil bought half of Humble for $17 million. Between 1918 and 1929 the fixed assets of Humble Oil expanded from $13 million to $233 million, with much capital assistance provided by Standard and allied East Coast banks. Humble Oil became the largest U.S. producer of crude oil.[8]

During the decade of the 1920s Houston's economy was maturing, with services and manufactured products critical to the oil industry increasingly being provided by local companies. Oil-equipment and oil-services companies were financed to a substantial degree by Texas capital, and most of these support companies escaped take over by northern corporations. Major gas-pipeline companies also were established in the 1920s in Houston.[9]

At the beginning of the Great Depression Houston was a growing but still modest manufacturing center. Harris County had nearly 500 manu-

facturing plants, most of them in oil-related industries, with 26,000 employees. Still, manufacturing was not as dominant in Houston as in other manufacturing cities. Indeed, in the nation as a whole there were 30 percent more people employed in manufacturing than in sales. In Houston, by contrast, the reverse was true; there were more sales workers than manufacturing workers.[10] In addition, Houston already had a large number of clerical, managerial, and professional workers employed in a growing number of office facilities. From the 1920s Houston was a complex city occupationally, with a large administrative and professional work force, a large manufacturing work force, and a large commercial work force. The city more than doubled its population—to 292,352—between 1920 and 1930, while the population of Harris County and surrounding counties was approaching half a million. In this decade Houston passed Dallas and San Antonio to become the largest city in Texas.

The growing blue-collar work force in Houston was substantially composed of blacks and Hispanics. Black workers had done a considerable portion of the "dirty work" in the city from the 1850s to the 1930s. Although rigidly segregated, blacks established large and important neighborhoods by World War I, developments that we document in more detail in Chapter 5. In addition, by the 1920s the Mexican-American population in Houston had reached into the thousands and provided much of the labor for Houston's escalating growth. We detail the growth and significance of Hispanic Houstonians in Chapter 6.

The Era of State-Assisted Oligopoly Capitalism:
The 1930s and 1940s

Until the 1930s most examples of government intervention in Houston involved the local growth coalition (local business and development interests, combined with local government officials) working to boost Texas cities or improve the local infrastructure. But in the 1930s and 1940s some new and extraordinary types of state intervention, including "social capital" expenditures, gave a major impetus to the economies of Texas cities —particularly Houston. The Houston economic base became integrally linked to several levels of government in this period.

New Oil Fields   During the 1930s new oil fields were regularly discovered in Texas. The extremely large East Texas oil field was developed in the early 1930s; by 1939 it included 26,000 wells. At first, most of the field was in the hands of the smaller oil companies, with just a fifth controlled by

major companies; by 1940 these control proportions were just the opposite. Much of the decision making about this newly discovered oil wealth was performed by oil companies with major subsidiaries in Houston. In 1935 just under half of all Texas oil was shipped through the Port of Houston. Houston had 1,200 oil companies and 300 oil supply houses. A variety of oil facilities, from refineries to office buildings, were the concrete embodiment of Houston's continuing oil boom. A *Fortune* magazine article noted that "without oil Houston would have been just another cotton town." [11] At that time it was estimated that the oil industry accounted for over half the jobs in the Houston area. Even during the depression, Houston continued to grow in jobs, people, office buildings, and residential subdivisions.

Between the 1920s and the 1940s a series of technological innovations in refining (e.g., catalytic cracking) increased the quantity and quality of gasoline extracted from crude oil. By 1941 the Gulf Coast (Texas and Louisiana) was the dominant oil refining region, with more than one-third of the total United States refining capacity. The Gulf Coast terrain was flat, permitting long pipelines to carry oil and gas from Texas, Oklahoma, and Louisiana oil fields to Gulf Coast refineries and to tankers at ports such as Houston along the Gulf Coast.[12] By the 1930s Houston was the nation's sixth-largest port, a major trading and shipping center in the Sunbelt. Cotton, lumber, and oil accounted for the rise in tonnage shipped from 1.3 million tons in 1919 to 27 million tons in 1941. Houston soon surpassed New Orleans as the dominant Gulf seaport. Its population continued to grow during the depression. Houston had become the major regional metropolis, a central node connecting neighboring Gulf Coast cities.

Government Intervention in the Economy   The government's role in supporting Houston's development became more conspicuous in the 1930s and 1940s. As was the case with many northern cities, the essential infrastructure of Houston was expanded greatly in the 1930s with substantial federal aid.

The provision of large-scale aid to Houston in this period was facilitated by the vertical ties between the local growth coalition in Texas and the federal government. The Texas political delegation was a powerful lobby on Capital Hill. John Nance Garner, then vice president, had already represented Texas in Washington for many years. Sam Rayburn, another Texan, was the House majority leader and, later, Speaker of the House. One of the most important Texans was Houstonian Jesse Jones, a man at the center of the local growth coalition with strong links to the federal purse. He became Roosevelt's head of the Reconstruction Finance Corpo-

ration (RFC) in the 1930s and served as FDR's secretary of commerce. During the 1930s New Deal money was critical to the building of Houston's infrastructure. Federal money was used to construct public buildings, including the city hall, parks, monuments, schools, and roads. More than a million dollars in federal funds were provided for further improvements to the Houston ship channel, and $1.2 million was provided for a new city hall. With development guided by the growth coalition and with millions in federal government capital for roads, schools, and bridges, a substantial urban infrastructure was built.[13] To a substantial degree, these federal expenditures enhanced the profitability of Houston's private industrial and real estate corporations as well as the livability of the city in general.

Corporate Executives Work for Government Intervention   A remarkable example of state intervention in a market economy can be seen in the Texas oil industry in the 1930s. The rapid development of the East Texas oil field brought Houston-based and other oil companies, small and large, into vigorous competition. Prices dropped to very low levels, with large quantities of oil pumped out at rates of production that violated Texas state laws. By the early 1930s major oil company executives urged the federal government to set oil pumping quotas in the East Texas field. Federal agents were sent to Texas to help the Texas Railroad Commission (the Texas oil-regulation agency) bring order to the oil fields. This intervention, and continuing federal support for the prorationing of pumping among the oil companies by the Texas Railroad Commission, operated from the 1930s to the 1970s to protect the petroleum industry from a more competitive market in oil production. Houston-based companies prospered under government protection from open competition, and their prosperity ensured that Houston would continue to grow during and after the depression.[14]

World War II: The Economy Expands   By the 1940s the federal government was a source of social investment capital for oil-related industrial development. During World War II more than $250 million in government-provided capital was poured into private and joint private-public oil-related enterprises in the Gulf Coast area. In particular, federal expenditures flowed to the petrochemical industry; aviation fuel and synthetic rubber were essential to the war effort.[15] While a trinity of resources—iron ore, coal, and limestone—had brought the steel age to Pittsburgh, the lineup of raw materials was different for Houston's petrochemical industry: "a trilogy of oil and gas, sulfur, and fresh water." [16] Refinery by-products from making gasoline became feedstocks for making petrochemicals which is

why petrochemical plants are often located near oil refineries; indeed, many chemical plants are owned by oil companies. The Port of Houston became a major shipping avenue for petrochemical products, and for that reason production sites were located there.

The newly developing petrochemical industry at first served war interests. Soon, however, it became a major Houston industry producing commercial products. Crude oil and natural gas are raw materials for a huge array of petrochemical products considered necessary for a modern industrial society—asphalt and fuel oils as well as a variety of plastics and other synthetic products.

Federal investment also took the form of aid for oil and gas production and distribution. During World War II, at a cost of $142 million, the Roosevelt administration built two major oil pipelines, called the "Big Inch" and the "Little Inch," to carry oil products from Texas to the East Coast. The "Big Inch" pipeline was built from the East Texas oil field to New York's refining areas; Houston's Humble Oil Company played a role in that pipeline project. Humble Oil was also the leading U.S. supplier of oil and gas feedstocks; the Humble Baytown refinery had a 140,000-barrel-a-day capacity, making it the largest in the United States. During the war Humble Oil laboratories did electronics work as well, designing radar and other detection equipment.[17]

The range of state aid for industrial and urban development in the greater Houston area was remarkably broad, from aid for infrastructure projects and social capital for the petrochemical and oil-pipeline companies to regulation interference at the request of oil companies. A recognition of the extent of state aid in this era of oligopoly capitalism is missing from mainstream urban analyses of the Sunbelt, while uneven-development theorists have paid more attention to the role of the state. Given the substantial state intervention in the Houston and Texas economies, it is not surprising that the 1930s and 1940s were eras of growth in jobs and population and thus in relative prosperity. By the 1940s Houston had seen the completion of its first modern airport; and from 1937 to 1942 a large amount of capital —$100 million—went into real estate development projects in Houston.

The Era of State-Aided Oligopoly Capitalism:
Recent Decades

After World War II Houston began a long boom fueled by the rising national demand for oil and oil products. Demand for asphalt, jet fuel, plastics, and other petrochemicals increased dramatically. Earlier, state aid for

the oil, petrochemical, and pipeline companies helped place them in an advantageous position to capture part of the postwar boom. State regulation of the Texas-Houston oil industry helped guarantee stability in the generation of products and profits. The Texas Gulf Coast became a major target of outside investment capital. Houston was becoming nationally eminent in its "oil function." An ever-increasing number of transportation companies—including truck, pipeline, and shipping companies—had grown up around greater Houston's oil and petrochemical complexes. There was continued growth in steel, aluminum, metal fabrication, oil-tool, and construction companies. And in the 1950s the city's population grew by 57 percent, to nearly 1 million by the end of the decade.

Government aid for the oil industry has continued to foster its prosperity from World War II to the present. In the late 1950s the profitability of oil companies concentrating on production in the United States was further enhanced by state action. In 1959 President Eisenhower set quotas for imported oil, limiting oil imports to 12 percent of domestic oil production, a decision considered necessary for national defense. This cost American consumers of oil and oil-related products an estimated \$50 billion in the 1959–1969 decade. Oil and gas price increases have regularly stimulated the metropolitan Houston economy, as was the case during the 1950s and 1960s.[18] In addition, federal tax subsidies for oil companies, such as the oil depletion allowance, and favorable tax treatment of income earned overseas contributed to a healthy profit structure for the major oil companies over several decades. These actions also facilitated expanded investment in Houston's economy.

Moreover, in the 1960–1980 period there were other important examples of federal support for Houston's economy. The National Aeronautic and Space Administration (NASA) complex came to Houston in the 1960s after Houston's growth coalition, which included prominent business leaders and local politicians, prevailed in competition with other cities. Land for the NASA complex was donated by Humble Oil (Exxon), whose nearby real estate holdings increased in value as a result. This type of large-scale, capital-intensive, state-aided project was—and is—attractive to Houston's business elite.

Houston participated to a lesser extent in such government programs as Model Cities, as we will explore more fully in the next chapter. In recent decades most government assistance has gone into road building, sewer facilities, and airport construction. About 60 percent of federal aid in the 1970s and 1980s went for these infrastructure projects, with 40 percent going for social services. Houston's pro-business growth coalition has de-

emphasized federal social welfare programs, particularly those benefiting low-income and minority residents.

Houston and Restructuring in the Oil Industry   In the late 1960s and early 1970s several major oil companies shifted more of their important subsidiaries to the Houston area or buttressed their existing operations there. The British-Dutch Shell Oil company located its U.S. administrative headquarters there, and Exxon concentrated more of its national administrative and research operations in the Houston area. Gulf, Texaco, and Conoco also located or expanded major national subsidiaries there. Houston's national and international importance as an oil center was now solidified. Previously dispersed oil company offices were consolidated in larger offices in a few key cities, including Houston. Production operations, and even some consumer and marketing operations, were likewise consolidated in Houston.

Of the nation's 35 largest oil companies, most have located major administrative, research, and production facilities in the greater Houston area. In addition to these giants, there are nearly 500 other oil and gas companies, and hundreds of geological firms, petroleum engineering firms, drilling contractors, geophysical contractors, supply and transportation companies, law firms, and accounting firms serving Houston's oil and gas companies. One result of the recentralization of production has been the migration of a large number of white-collar workers to the Houston area.[19] Although numerous major oil companies now have important domestic subsidiaries in Houston, most of these subsidiaries are still dependent on northern headquarters for major investment decisions. Oil company executives tend to be promoted from Houston subsidiaries to New York (sometimes via overseas assignments), rather than vice versa.

Concentration of control over the Texas oil industry continued through the 1960s and 1970s so that in the late 1970s there were about 5,000 oil companies in crude oil production in Texas, yet just six large companies—Exxon, Gulf, Shell, Conoco, Chevron, and Mobil—produced 37 percent of the oil in Texas. Most of the Texas production was in the hands of only 15 companies. Other aspects of the oil business were even more centralized. Exxon, Gulf, Shell, Mobil, Phillips, Chevron, Amoco, and Sun Oil refined two-thirds of the crude oil in Texas.[20]

Housing the Oil Industry   The expansion of Houston's oil industry since the 1960s has led to a conspicuous increase in the number of its people and office buildings. Houston's population grew from just under a million

in 1960 to an estimated 1.7 million in the early 1980s, an increase of more than 70 percent. The metropolitan area grew to more than 3 million people in the same period. In addition, between 1970 and 1981 a total of 361 large office buildings (of 100,000 square feet or more) were built in the Houston area, more than 80 percent of *all* existing large office buildings ever built in the city. By 1986 the number had grown to 485 major structures.[21]

Many of these 485 buildings are administrative centers where the executive and clerical offices of oil and gas corporations—as well as those of related service firms—make and implement the critical decisions shaping local, national, and global oil and gas operations. From Houston's office towers oil company executives coordinate exploration, leasing, drilling, and research aspects of the oil and gas industry. Nearby numerous oil refining facilities and petrochemical plants with close linkages to pipelines and pipeline companies make use of oil and gas feedstocks. For the 1970s and 1980s the major aspects of this Houston-based oil and gas industry can be distinguished as follows:

1. units of large corporations controlling the discovery of oil and gas, particularly research, leasing, and exploration units;
2. units of large corporations and smaller companies controlling the drilling of oil wells;
3. subsidiaries of large companies and independent companies controlling oil and gas transportation (e.g., pipelines, tankers);
4. other oil service companies, such as fire-suppression companies, law firms, and accounting firms;
5. oil-tool companies manufacturing machinery, drilling equipment, and construction equipment;
6. metal fabrication companies making pipe, storage tanks, and oil rigs;
7. subsidiaries of large corporations and independent companies refining oil into gasoline and feedstocks;
8. petrochemical companies processing feedstocks into plastics and similar products;
9. subsidiaries of large oil companies and independent companies marketing oil and gas products, including ad agencies and service stations.

Some of these operations are predominantly white-collar and are housed in office towers; others are located in refineries and petrochemical plants with large blue-collar work forces. In 1978 Houston was ranked as the fourth-largest manufacturing center in the United States—behind Chicago,

Detroit, and Los Angeles—in value of manufacturing shipments, and it was first in new capital expenditures in manufacturing.[22] Yet in 1980 about 57 percent of the Houston standard metropolitan statistical area (SMSA) work force was employed in white-collar jobs (managerial, professional, clerical, and sales), which was close to the proportion of white-collar workers in Philadelphia (58 percent).

Oil, Petrochemical, and Economic Growth within the City   The distribution of office towers in Houston and the recent explosion in the number of such buildings illustrate two key aspects of economic growth and development within the city of Houston itself—recent large-scale development in the city and the decentralized character of internal growth since World War II. Oil and petrochemicals have been regularly linked to this spatial development.

In 1910 Houston was a modest city of 78,000 people. It had a central-city area with a small downtown of low-rise office buildings and shops, railings to tie horses, and extensive railroad yards and repair facilities north of the downtown area. While there were a few residential areas farther out, much of the city was within a mile of the downtown area. In the 1920s the construction of major oil-related industrial facilities such as oil refineries along the ship channel (which extended southeast of the downtown area) triggered an expansion of the city to the southeast. Blue-collar residential developments were built on this east side, often near the refineries. After a lull in construction in the early 1930s, by the late 1930s and 1940s industrial development on the southeast side was extensive. Also in this period there was some expansion of residential development to the west, as residential communities close to downtown such as West University grew to house the white-collar workers (e.g., scientists and technicians) working for oil-related firms in downtown office buildings. Since the 1920s and 1930s there has been a tendency for blue-collar workers to be housed on the east side of the city (as well as the minority workers discussed in Chapters 5 and 6) and for white-collar workers to be housed on the west side.

Houston expanded outward after World War II, particularly with the construction of major highways running north, south, and west from the city. Houston had some of the first divided, four-lane roads in the Sunbelt. These highways, together with an absence of any commitment to a significant mass transit system, meant that Houston was clearly a car-dominated city. Houston's roadway system is one of the most extensive in the United States and has consumed a large share of the highway funds

spent in Texas. The local growth coalition has worked aggressively over the decades since 1940 to see that a major highway grid was put into place. Given this highway-centered transportation system, Houston's large-scale real estate development has radiated out along this grid in a decentralized pattern.

In recent years urban demographers have discussed the deconcentration and decentralization trends of many U.S. metropolitan areas in the last two decades. But these trends were under way in Houston as early as the 1950s, with the construction of office and shopping sites in a number of dispersed areas far from the downtown center. This large-scale development began in the southwest corridor in the 1950s. Today this corridor has considerably more office building and shopping center space than the entire area of downtown Houston. Many residential subdivisions and apartment buildings were subsequently built in this corridor. Moreover, in the 1960s the arrival of NASA well to the south of Houston generated an expansion of office, shopping center, and residential developments to the south and southeast of the city.

By the late 1970s there were more than a dozen business-activity centers scattered around the city, in addition to the downtown area. Much related commercial real estate development has taken place in the 1970s and 1980s. As we noted in the previous section of this chapter, the office space has been dominated by firms tied directly or indirectly to Houston's oil and petrochemical companies, including service firms in law, accounting, and real estate.[23]

The highly decentralized character of business and manufacturing activity in Houston is distinctive among U.S. cities. Many older cities have seen a pattern of internal development in which decaying central cities are abandoned by businesses for suburban areas. But in spatial terms Houston is a very new city. Most of its built environment, from suburbs to office towers, has been constructed in the last 20 to 30 years. So the pattern is not slow expansion out from a troubled central city. From the 1950s Houston has been built up by its developers and other real estate actors in a decentralized fashion. There is no large, decaying downtown area, and no slow expansion outward over several decades has occurred. Rather, in a short period a polynucleate city has been built up, with only a modest portion of the city's construction dating from before the 1940s. This polynucleate development has resulted from several factors, including the massive freeway system facilitating accessibility to all parts of the city (at least before the large traffic jams developed), the lack of restrictions on development

(e.g., *no* zoning laws), and the high velocity of investment-capital flowing into the city's large-scale construction projects in the late postwar period.

If one were to compare Houston with major cities in the Frostbelt, this oil-related decentralized pattern of city development would stand out as unique. Houston's growth has been linked directly to changes in the oil industry. Locating oil refineries along the ship channel fueled the boom of the 1920s and 1930s. New petrochemical industries, linked to the war effort, spurred another boom to the east and southeast after World War II. And the location of oil-related companies in Houston since the 1950s, together with the sharp rise in the price of oil in the 1970s, accelerated the development boom in many parts of the city. Since the 1950s there has been industrial and real estate development all around the city. Unlike Cleveland, New York, and Pittsburgh, Houston is too new to have areas of substantial industrial or real estate decline. Indeed, the expansion of the city has been so rapid that there are large vacant areas within the city available for future development. So far, Houston's many real estate development projects have been built on vacant land or have been built where nondecaying construction already existed. An example of the latter is the huge project called Greenway Plaza, built five miles from downtown Houston in the southwest corridor. Good-quality houses in four residential subdivisions were bulldozed or moved off the land to make way for the new and "higher" land use. Thus Houston has seen very little of the well-documented investment/disinvestment process typical of central cities in the North. Today the central-city area, with the exception of a few major private projects like Greenway Plaza and a few highway projects, has the same broad land-use pattern it had two decades ago.

There has been a limited amount of gentrification in the central city. In addition, the east-side minority areas (see Chapters 5 and 6 for details) have expanded in size, but large numbers of minority residents have not been displaced by public or private urban renewal programs. Indeed, Houston has had *no* public urban renewal program, the type of program often linked to major disinvestment and residential shifts in Frostbelt cities (see Chapter 3). In the downtown area new office buildings have frequently replaced older office buildings and department stores built since 1940, but there have been no large-scale clearance programs there.

One major problem for investors in the 1980s has been the overbuilding that took place in the last decade. In 1986 about 30 percent of the office space in the city was unoccupied. The downturn in the world oil economy resulted in bankrupt oil companies and massive employee layoffs. Many

developers of *new* buildings and of *new* residential subdivisions are in financial difficulty because of shifts in the world oil economy, a topic to which we now turn.

The International Oil Industry   In the 1960s and 1970s Houston became a technology-distribution center for the world's oil and gas market system. With the discovery of major Middle Eastern oil fields in the 1960s, advanced oil technologies were needed in the Middle East. Houston companies have been important in the development of other oil fields from the North Sea to Malaysia and Indonesia.[24] The growing demand for Houston products and services has kept employment growing and generated a boom mentality. The relationship between Houston's growth and prosperity and economic shifts in the larger capitalist world-market system can be seen clearly in events surrounding OPEC. In 1973 the OPEC nations gained control over their crude oil, and the once-dominant major oil companies became suppliers of technology and marketing agents for OPEC oil. U.S. oil company profits on Middle Eastern oil fell, but the sharp rise in world oil prices brought great increases in profits on oil controlled elsewhere.[25] As a result, in the 1973–1975 recession, employment in goods-producing industries dropped 6 percent in the Dallas/Fort Worth area but grew by 18 percent in Houston, particularly because its nonelectrical machinery and metals firms make materials for the oil and gas industry. The rise in OPEC oil prices in 1973–1974 boosted oil exploration and drilling, thus stimulating the Houston economy. Between 1968 and 1980 the percentage of Houston employment in oil exploration and drilling and oil-field machinery expanded.[26]

However, the rise in oil prices did have a major negative impact on one dimension of the Houston economy. Prior to the 1973–1974 price rise, a diversification trend was under way in the Houston area, with growing investment in nonoil industries and projects (e.g., real estate projects). But with the sharp rise in the price of oil, oil companies and allied bankers moved away from this diversification to a heavier emphasis on investments in oil-related projects. In the late 1970s there was yet another rise in the price of oil, which again stimulated the oil companies to overinvest in and overproduce oil and gas. As a result, the downturn in oil prices in the early 1980s caught many companies with large inventories of oil and oil supplies. Oil-tool companies had overproduced such items as drilling bits, and the recession meant a large surplus for them. Moreover, the downturn caused some oil companies to lay people off in order to cut costs and thus to improve their cash flow; fearing takeovers by other companies, some

oil executives tried to improve their cash flow in order to bring their own stock prices up, staving off outside takeover attempts. Sharply increased unemployment in Houston was the result.

The close ties between Houston and major cities in Latin America, the Middle East, and the Far East can be seen in the substantial international trade passing through the Port of Houston. In 1981 more than $26 billion in exports and imports flowed through the Houston customs district. By the early 1980s Houston ranked second among ports in the United States in total cargo tonnage and in foreign trade. Oil was by far the number one commodity imported at the Port of Houston. The next two major categories of imports were steel products and automobiles and transportation equipment. The number one export is construction, mining, and oil-field machinery. Unmilled grain and organic chemicals rank high as well. Houston relies heavily on imported oil, steel, and autos; and it primarily exports agricultural products and products from its oil and petrochemical industries.[27] The large population increases in Houston between 1960 and 1980 were closely linked to the city's role in the international oil market.

The important national and international economic developments for Houston's growth and prosperity were highlighted in the early 1980s. While Houston's oil and gas economy buoyed the city up during the depression and most postwar recessions, the 1980s brought a different scenario. The 1981–1983 recession hit Houston hard; between early 1982 and mid-1983 economic activity declined and unemployment rose significantly. The recession saw Houston's industrial production fall more rapidly than the national average; in addition, the unemployment rate grew more rapidly in Houston than in the nation, hitting 9.7 percent in 1983, up sharply from 1981. By 1986 unemployment had grown to just under 15 percent, well above Houston's depression-level figure. Problems in the Texas oil industry came to the surface when OPEC members were forced to reduce oil prices in the 1980s. The drop in oil prices brought substantial production cutbacks and employee layoffs in the greater Houston area. Refinery use in Texas declined from 91 percent of capacity in the late 1970s to less than 70 percent of capacity in 1983. The governor of Texas told some oil-field workers that they should train for other jobs.[28] After a brief and partial recovery, the city (and Texas) went into an even more severe economic recession in 1984–1987, a situation we discuss in the final chapter.

The international decline in oil prices was not the only factor affecting Houston's oil economy. U.S. demand for oil was slowing dramatically. Until 1975 the growth in U.S. energy demand was similar to the growth in gross national product (GNP). Since that time, in part because of the

sharply higher oil prices coming into place in the 1972–1975 period, the growth in energy demand has been less than real GNP growth in the United States. In addition to a decline in demand, the Texas Gulf Coast oil and petrochemical industries have also faced the problem of declining oil production. Texas oil reserves are gradually being exhausted; oil production peaked in the 1960s. By the mid-1970s, 4.4 million barrels of oil a day were produced for Houston and other Gulf Coast refineries. By the early 1980s the 50 Texas refineries were generally importing a third of the oil feedstocks they were processing, a figure that has been as high as 46 percent. The comparable figure was 2 percent in 1972. Processing the heavier foreign oil being imported was costly; it required several billion dollars in expenditures to retool Texas refining capacity to handle its deficiencies.[29] These changes are signals that Texas is an aging oil province.

Conclusion

The business climate of Houston has facilitated growth. The local government seeks federal government aid to assist business-oriented development. The growth coalition of business and development interests has worked through local government to secure lower taxes and government subsidies for infrastructure projects. The case of Houston illustrates the class-structured character of growth coalitions in cities. That the benefits they bring often disproportionately accrue to corporations and upper-income groups has been documented not only for Houston but also for metropolitan New York and other major U.S. cities.[30]

It is also erroneous to view cities such as Houston as part of some inevitable filtering or "catching up" process. Understanding Houston is not a question of discovering a recently developed urban economy with a primitive-economy past. Since its days as a regional commercial center in 1900, Houston has had a developed economy. Even before the discovery of oil Houston enjoyed major economic growth.[31] Indeed, it was a thriving cotton, timber, and railroad center by 1900. The discovery of oil and the expansion of the oil industry accelerated growth in a city already experiencing an economic advance. Oil came to Houston in part because Houston already had a developed transportation-commerce infrastructure. And Houston's oil economy did not spring suddenly into being in the 1960s; it began in the 1920s. Most urban analysts have not dealt adequately with the cumulative character of development in the economic base of cities.

Sunbelt city development does not necessarily converge in a rational

way with Frostbelt city development. Pursuit of profit and efficiency at the firm level can mean irrational and uneven development between regions, between cities within a region, and within cities. The first wave of oil-related corporate investments flowed to Houston in the 1908–1929 period and gradually built up the city's oil-economy base. These investments came later in time than comparable investments in the iron-steel industries of Pittsburgh or the many industries of New York. Yet major oil-related investments were in place in Houston long before 1950–1980, the period most analysts of Sunbelt cities emphasize.

This spurring of oil-gas investment had as much to do with private corporate decisions shaping the U.S. transportation system—that is, decisions creating an auto- and truck-centered system as opposed to a European-type combination (electric) mass transit and auto system—than with the good business climate in the Gulf Coast area. The expansion of investment in auto-centered Detroit spurred investment in the greater Houston area in the 1920s, the most rapid growth period in Houston's history.

In the regional-urban economics and urban ecology literatures there are various discussions of a hierarchy of U.S. cities, with emphasis on hierarchies within a region. Berry distinguishes between the self-sustaining growth of key metropolitan areas and the "hand-me-down" metropolitan periphery, which gets second-hand growth from the search for lower production costs.[32] Yet this concept of an urban hierarchy within or between regions does not fully capture relationships such as that between Houston and Detroit. This relationship is not primarily one of filtering or convergence. Rather, this linkage is one whereby economic development in the auto industry in Detroit fuels raw materials development a thousand miles away in Texas.

Numerous urban analysts portray northern cities as failing to capture the new post–World War II industries that lie at the heart of Sunbelt dynamism. This failure is attributed by some mainstream analysts to poor business climates and by some uneven-development analysts to the inertia of northern capitalists locked into existing investments. Yet Houston's dynamic oil and gas industry is not a new leading-edge industry of the postwar period. As we have seen, oil and gas production and refining became the major industrial base of Houston in the 1915–1940 period. Neither New York nor Pittsburgh nor any northern city had a chance to secure this industry because the oil and petrochemical industries located, as classical location theorists would suggest, near critical materials. A related problem with these explanations of Sunbelt growth is the excessive attention to certain types of manufacturing industries, particularly defense-related

electronics and new high-tech industries located in a few Sunbelt cities. Somewhat older high-tech industries such as oil refining or petrochemicals are slighted.

Houston's development also illustrates the role of local growth coalitions in city development. Houston has long had a successful growth coalition, including capitalist actors from real estate, banking, oil, and other businesses, as well as top government officials (see Chapters 3 and 4). Coordinated through the Houston Chamber of Commerce, the coalition has worked effectively through local, state, and federal governments to bring social investment capital to Houston.

After this overview of Houston's emergence as a major metropolitan center, we now turn to an examination of the political and social dimensions of Houston's growth and decline as well as to its impact on Houston's minority communities.

3

City and Suburban Politics:
Changing Patterns of
Political Determination

Local business officials sometimes boast about Houston's independence from outside governmental assistance or direction. The standard fare has been, "We don't need or want federal dollars or the conditions that accompany them!" Houston has thus come to be seen as an anomaly among large cities, eschewing federal aid while other cities were becoming more dependent. In contrast to this image, however, in Houston, as in cities throughout the nation, the federal presence has historically been part of the growth and development. As we saw in Chapter 2, one element of Houston's politics is the federal government, and in this chapter we examine how the federal presence in Houston has evolved. Before we discuss the role of the federal government in Houston, however, we examine city and suburban politics to determine how these relations, as well as those between Houston and the federal government, have affected the city's growth.

Metropolitan areas in the United States are typically "crazy-quilt" patterns of governments, with one city's limits blurring into the next, and with the suburban sprawl of housing tracts, commercial strips, mammoth shopping centers, and units of local governments crisscrossing the urban landscape. What stands out in this arrangement is the encirclement of central cities by small, suburban, city fiefdoms. While the city of St. Louis—surrounded by more than 100 municipalities—is an often cited example of the "locked–in" city, the pattern is noted in other cities as well.

The territorial arrangement of governments in the metropolis affects the demographic, socioeconomic, and political characteristics of the area. Governmental fragmentation is seen as one of the root causes of central-city economic decline, polarization of racial and ethnic groups, decline in the quality of inner-city life, and service disparities between city dwellers and suburbanites. When a central city can no longer grow territorially, it

usually becomes increasingly segregated socioeconomically and racially. Its tax base erodes, its quality of life diminishes, and its service costs increase.

Most central cities resemble the pattern depicted here with variation only in the extent of their territorial constriction. Houston is less territorially confined than older cities of the Northeast and Midwest. Thus, the chief characteristic of the Houston area at present is the population, territorial, and political dominance of the city of Houston over other cities and areas in the metropolitan area—a condition explained in large part by Houston's age and its stage of development within the metropolitan area. Houston is a young city; unlike older cities that developed during the pre–World War I industrialization, it grew much later.[1] Older "industrial" cities tended to lose population between 1950 and 1970, while young cities like Houston grew.[2] The differences in population growth or decline are paralleled by city-suburban cleavages, which are more pronounced in older cities, and by sharp differences in the developmental characteristics of young cities (e.g., older cities ceased to expand territorially, whereas young cities annexed large amounts of new land in recent decades).[3]

Like other metropolitan areas, the Houston region is overlaid with many local governments. Houston is part of Harris County, and overlaying the city's borders are countywide hospital and flood-control districts and an areawide metropolitan transit authority. Jutting in and out of the city's limits are four junior college districts and 19 independent school districts. Houston also is encircled by about 400 special-purpose districts, usually called municipal utility districts (MUDs) but sometimes referred to as "developer" districts because they serve small subdivisions and/or commercial and industrial developments in unincorporated areas.

This array of governmental units coexists with Houston and 32 cities located in or partly in Harris County. A cursory glance at a map of the Houston metropolitan area (see Map 3.1) shows that Houston is the municipal giant overshadowing the other suburban cities in the county. Furthermore, as explained below, Houston's dominance is strengthened by legal, economic, and political realities.

Houston's Territorial Dominance

State law provides Houston with an extraterritorial jurisdiction (ETJ) that extends five miles from its corporate limits.[4] Houston's ETJ exceeds 2,000 square miles—an area larger than the state of Rhode Island—and covers all of Harris County and portions of six adjacent counties. Within its ETJ,

Map 3.1   The Houston metropolitan area

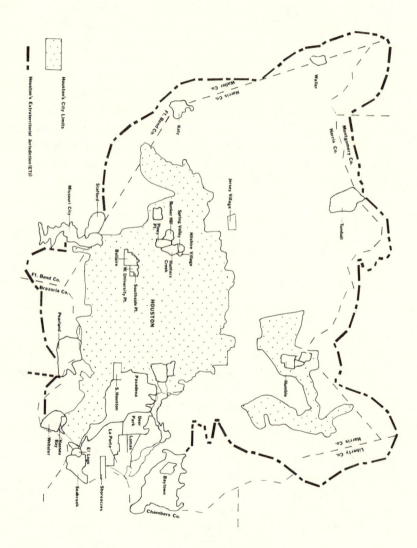

Houston's City Limits

Houston's Extraterritorial Jurisdiction (ETJ)

Houston has exclusive authority to annex by simple ordinance without voter approval, to prevent new incorporations, and to consent to the formation of municipal utility districts. Houston enjoys this control over the ETJ but is not obligated to provide services until it annexes.

As shown in Table 3.1, only Pasadena and Baytown have populations (112,560 and 56,923, respectively) that afford them a substantive ETJ, but the geography of these two cities constricts that legal authority. Along with other cities to the east and southeast of Houston, Pasadena and Baytown are almost entirely hemmed in between Houston and the Gulf Coast. Elsewhere in Harris County, 13 cities are enclaves within Houston and do not have ETJs. Five other cities are forced to negotiate with Houston (or go to court) if they want to expand, since they are encircled by Houston's ETJ. The three cities to the south can grow into other counties but not into Houston's ETJ.

Population changes in incorporated and unincorporated areas of Harris County between 1970 and 1980 illustrate the consequences of Houston's territorial control over other Harris County cities. Almost all the growth in the urban population took place either in the city of Houston or in its ETJ. Harris County's population increased by 667,632 during the 1970s. The city of Houston gained 51.7 percent (or 345,057) of the total. The unincorporated portions of the county—practically all of them in Houston's ETJ—gained 37.9 percent (or 252,901) of the total. Houston and its ETJ thus acquired 89.6 percent of the area's growth, while the 32 other cities in the area attained a meager 10.4 percent of the total (69,674). Since Houston restricts the territorial growth of the area of other cities, their populations must expand within fixed boundaries. Houston, on the other hand, has enormous potential for growth, not only within its corporate limits but also in its vast ETJ. Yet any attempt of the city to grow through annexation of adjacent areas must meet federal guidelines imposed in the 1970s to prevent the dilution of the city's minority power through the annexation of predominantly white areas. For example, in the mid-1980s the mayor's office proposed the annexation of a northern suburban area, arguing that the city's minority population had sufficiently increased to allow the annexation of the predominantly white area.

Service responsibilities for the unincorporated portions of the metropolitan area rest largely with three entities: Harris County, independent school districts, and MUDs. Each provides services within its sphere of authorities without interfering with Houston's eventual control over its ETJ.

Table 3.1 Selected characteristics of cities in Harris County
and their territorial relationship to the city of Houston

City	Population[a]	Legal authority	Form of government	ETJ authority[b] (miles)	Land area (sq. miles)[c]
Houston	1,594,086	HR	MC	5	556.4
Surrounded by Houston					
Bellaire	14,950	HR	CM	1	3.6
Bunker Hill Village	3,750	GL	MC	1/2	1.5
Galena Park	9,879	HR	MC	1	4.9
Hedwig Village	2,506	GL	MC	1/2	.9
Hilshire Village	621	GL	MC	1/2	.1
Humble	6,729	HR	MC	1	9.5
Hunter's Creek Village	4,215	GL	MC	1/2	.5
Jacinto City	8,953	GL	MC	1	1.8
Piney Point	2,958	GL	MC	1/2	3.2
South Houston	13,293	GL	MC	1	2.9
Southside Place	1,366	GL	MC	1/2	.3
Spring Valley Village	3,353	GL	MC	1/2	1.4
West University Place	12,010	HR	CM	1	2.0
Encircled by ETJ					
Jersy Village	4,084	GL	MC	1/2	2.1
Katy	4,475	GL	MC	1/2	3.6
Pearland	13,248	HR	CM	1	15.8
Tomball	3,996	GL	MC	1/2	.8
Waller	1,241	GL	MC	1/2	.9
Abutted by Houston					
Deer Park	22,648	HR	CM	1	15.4
El Lago	3,129	GL	MC	1/2	.3
La Porte	14,062	HR	MC	1	16.2
Lomax	2,964	GL	MC	1/2	5.2
Morgan Point	428	GL	MC	1/2	2.2
Nassau Bay	4,526	GL	CM	1/2	1.7
Pasadena	112,560	HR	MC	5	42.5
Seabrook	4,670	GL	MC	1/2	6.3
Shoreacres	1,260	GL	MC	1/2	1.9
Taylor Lake	3,669	GL	MC	1/2	.5
Webster	2,168	GL	MC	1/2	3.1

Table 3.1   (Continued)

City	Population[a]	Legal authority	Form of government	ETJ authority[b] (miles)	Land area (sq. miles)[c]
Can grow outside ETJ					
Baytown	56,923	HR	CM	3 1/2	25.4
Missouri City	24,533	HR	MC	2	27.5
Stafford	4,755	GL	MC	1/2	9.2
	(86,211)				(62.1)

[a] *Source: 1980 Census of Population and Housing.*

[b] The ETJs listed are defined by the Municipal Annexation Act of 1963. In practice, those cities surrounded by Houston do not have ETJs; those encircled by Houston's ETJ must negotiate with Houston if they wish to expand; those abutted by Houston are limited because of restrictions on landscape.

[c] *Source: Houston and Harris County Atlas* (Houston: Key Maps, 1980).

HR: Home Rule
GL: General Law
MC: Mayor-Council
CM: Council-Manager

Harris County   Under its state constitutional authority, Harris County functions as an administrative arm of the state government. The array of administrative tasks that county officials are obligated to perform define the purpose and scope of their action. These generally supplement and support, not supplant, city functions. The perception on the part of Harris County Commissioners is that the city is part of the county insofar as county services are concerned. Indeed, county officials do not interfere with the city of Houston's political objectives when they operate the courts, supervise the jails, administer elections, build and maintain roads, establish libraries and parks, and tend to a bevy of housekeeping functions.

Independent School Districts   The structure of independent school districts in the Houston region diminishes responsibilities. Houston is a beneficiary of independent school districts, first, because its boundaries are not linked to school district boundaries. There are 22 independent school districts in Harris County, with 19 of these either inside Houston or crisscrossing its borders. As Houston has annexed new areas over the years, independent school districts have retained their existing territories. Even after Houston annexes, the districts continue to provide a structure of neighborhood or near-neighborhood schools, which makes Houston's annexations more palatable to suburbanites whose existing schools are not affected when brought within Houston's city boundaries.

Table 3.2 Number of water districts created and
district bond authorizations in Harris County for
selected years between 1949 and 1984

Years	Number of water districts created	Bond authorizations (in thousands)
1949–1954	27	10,107
1955–1960	39	32,477
1961–1966	46	32,968
1967–1972	187	352,447
1973–1978	140	681,015
1979–1984	118	1,111,772
	557	2,220,786

Source: Data for water district creation and bond authorizations compiled from Texas Water Commission records, 1949–
1984.

Independent school districts also shield Houston from some fiscal burdens. In other states, a major roadblock to annexation exists when "the
city government has responsibility for school financing without substantial
equalization assistance from the states." [5] Being able to move freely across
school district boundaries, the city of Houston does not have to assume
the fiscal burden of educational services. It avoids both the political problems associated with changing existing schools and the fiscal burden of
financing public education.

Municipal Utility Districts and Annexations Within the unincorporated
areas of Harris County there is a structure of special-purpose water conservation and reclamation districts that provide basic utilities to spur suburban development but do not threaten Houston with the prospect of being
surrounded by incorporated suburban governments. The Texas legislature
has authorized three types of districts for suburban development purposes:
fresh water supply districts (FWSDs), water control and improvement
districts (WCIDs), and municipal utility districts (MUDs). They benefit
Houston by financing services through bonds, which are the obligation of
neighborhood residents until the district is annexed by the city of Houston.
Houston's policy is to annex when the district's bond indebtedness is offset
by its ad valorem tax base.[6]

The significance of water districts to suburban development and to Houston's ability to capture suburban growth is shown in Table 3.2. From 1949
to 1984, 557 water districts were created in Harris County, and their col-

lective bond authorizations totaled about $2.221 billion. Today 407 active districts surround Houston, of which 359 are MUDs, 38 are WCIDs, and 10 are FWSDs.[7]

Closely related to MUD development are the city's annexations since World War II. Annexation has been a mainstay of city policy, expanding the tax base and capturing suburban growth.[8] The most dramatic annexations occurred in 1949 and 1956. Along with these large-scale annexations have come more modest expansions throughout the last 40 years. The city's size has increased by a factor of seven since 1948 (from 83.7 square miles to 556.4 square miles). Today Houston's territorial size is larger than the combined land areas of Chicago and Philadelphia.

Houston's Governmental Structure

Today Houston is governed by a strong mayor, an elected city controller, and a 14-member city council (9 members elected from districts and 5 members-at-large). The city government has evolved from a commission form of government.

When the Texas legislature granted Houston a home rule charter on March 18, 1905, it gave the city some distinctive governing qualities. A commission style of government, originated in nearby Galveston, was made the centerpiece of the new charter. The council was composed of the mayor and four aldermen. Elected every two years, the council members were mainly part-time, grass-roots amateurs. Executive and legislative functions were combined in the council. Each alderman was elected in one of four designated administrative positions: tax and land commissioner, fire commissioner, road and bridge commissioner, or water commissioner. The mayor was the weakest member of the council, yet the charter did provide the mayor with a veto and the power to appoint (with council approval) and remove department heads. The original charter reflected an implicit distrust of citizen oversight of official conduct (it had no recall article) and citizen input into policy-making (it had no initiative and referendum article). (Each article was added in a 1913 charter vote held shortly after a 1912 Home Rule Amendment was added to the Texas Constitution, giving cities the authority to alter their government structures without legislative approval.)

The commission years were administratively difficult: with legislative and administrative activities combined in a single body, the government had no effective leadership. On the one hand, the mayor had important ad-

ministrative power to appoint and remove department heads and to prepare the budget for ordinance-created departments as well as to delay council actions through the veto. On the other hand, the mayor was prevented from exercising any formal political or administrative leadership because the principal administrative functions were controlled by individual commissioners. In formulating the budget, for example, the mayor's power extended only to those departments created by ordinances; the bulk of city expenditures rested in the commissioner-led departments. Moreover, a majority of council could override the mayor's veto. Although the mayor voted with the council on a veto override, aldermen would not tolerate a mayor meddling in a commissioner's domain.

As department heads, the commissioners tended to defend the interests of their particular departments during the city council meetings. Budget sessions turned into logrolling contests in which alliances were established, and the department heads left out of these alliances were given budgetary leftovers. Since neither a chief executive nor a legislative body was independent of the existing departments, the commissioners tended to be unreceptive to new spending needs outside their limited responsibilities.

By the 1930s the commissioners' administration of city government became politicized and fragmented. Commissioners staffed their individual departments with persons loyal to their needs and interests, and mayors developed a spoils system of their own by appointing staff to ordinance-created departments. Thus, a patronage-laden bureaucracy emerged in Houston under the commission style of government.

In the early 1940s citizens reacted to the city government's inability to respond to polio and diptheria epidemics by placing charter reforms before the voters. They called for a professionally managed administration, with a manager as the key executive. The manager was to have almost exclusive power over departmental policies, personnel, and budgeting. The charter reform proposals limited the mayor's and the council's administrative powers. An eight-member council was advocated, and members were prohibited from exercising any administrative powers or heading any city departments. The mayor was to be the weak link in city government. Removal of the mayor's veto was the most telling divestment of the mayor's authority.

The plan was adopted, and Houston embarked on a five-year experiment with a professionally managed government. After World War II, however, a growth coalition of business and development interests and local political leaders wanted a government that supported private economic activities by doing what was minimally required. The private sector's opposition to

the city manager system was articulated by Oscar Holcombe. Holcombe was a fixture on the Houston governmental scene for 30 years, having been elected mayor 11 times. In 1946 he reemerged to capture the mayor's office. His campaign concentrated on two alleged failures of the city manager system: inadequate services and extravagant fiscal management. Holcombe won the election, and the city manager system was relegated to the scrap heap.

The city manager interlude offered a formal model for the direction of city affairs by an aggressive executive. It also provided a focal point for the opposition, which blamed the manager for all the city's ills. That target was not available in the commission-run government. The significance of the manager system, therefore, was to provide a framework for a strong executive and a weak council.

Houston's black and Hispanic communities have always been underrepresented in the political arena (see Chapters 5 and 6). The elimination of the all-white Democratic primary in the landmark 1944 U.S. Supreme Court *Smith* v. *Allwright* decision opened the doors to the black electorate. However, it took more than 14 years for the city to elect its first black to a public office. In 1958 Hattie Mae White was elected to the Houston independent school district (HISD) board; Asberry Butler was elected to the HISD board in 1964. Just one year after the passage of the Federal Voting Rights Act of 1965, two blacks were elected to state offices from Houston: Barbara Jordan to the Texas Senate and Curtis Graves to the House of Representatives. It was not until 1971, however, that Houston saw its first black on the city council.

Houston's minority electorate experienced steady growth in the 1970s. Moreover, black and Hispanic voters were demanding greater political representation from their own members. The minority community's voting strength was diluted by at-large council elections and the city's annexation of white suburban areas. In 1979 the U.S. Justice Department ruled that the city's annexations violated the Voting Rights Act and that the city had to modify its system of at-large elections. The Houston City Council was expanded from an 8-member council system in which all were elected at-large to the current 14-member council system in which 9 members are selected from districts and 5 elected at-large. The November 1979 election saw two blacks elected from districts, a third black elected at-large, and the first Hispanic elected to the Houston City Council.

The effect of abolishing the manager position was to make the mayor the central figure in city government. The extensive managerial authorities given to the manager in the 1942 charter were simply transferred to the mayor—but without council oversight attached. The focal point of city

governance and politics in the post–World War II era has been mayoral politics. In all facets of city government Houston's mayor has most of the powers of the classic strong mayor. The extent of mayoral control of city governance is best indicated in the relationship of the mayor's powers to those of the council, the controller, and the bureaucracy.

The council's powers since 1942 have been exclusively legislative; in the operations of city business, the council is subordinate to the mayor. The mayor organizes the legislative agenda, recommends policy, and casts a vote as a member of the council. Consequently, the mayor initiates and the council reacts. Even when the council is authorized to exercise control or oversight over the mayor, this power is limited. The council may approve all mayoral appointments to city departments and to boards and commissions, but if the mayor chooses to remove any of these officials, the council cannot interfere. Furthermore, the mayor can create and fill a number of high-paying executive staff jobs in the mayor's office without council approval. This allows the mayor to maintain direction over the city's business and its programs as well as over state and national programs that the city administers. While the council can alter any item recommended in the mayor's budget by increasing, decreasing, or omitting it, in practice this does not happen. The mayor prepares the budget; and with almost absolute control over the city's bureaucracy, the mayor can shape budget recommendations to suit his or her priorities. It was not until 1988 that a group of council members succeeded in passing their own budget plan for the city, one which faced a projected budget deficit of about $20 million for the end of fiscal year 1988.

In addition to being the legislative leader, the mayor is also the city's chief executive and administrator. The mayor performs the administrative functions of a strong city manager: hiring, firing, and overseeing the conduct of city business. Accordingly, the mayor's office has been expanded to match the increased administrative demands of the job.

The growth of the mayor's office bureaucracy is largely attributable to three factors. The sheer complexity of administering an ever-increasing city bureaucracy made a larger mayoral staff essential. The growth of national grant programs in the 1970s required a city administrative machinery in or closely associated with the mayor's office. Finally, mayoral staff appointments became patronage plums.

Constraints on the Mayor   The city controller, the only other elected city executive, has emerged as a watchdog over the mayor's activities. As such, the controller is now the second most powerful official in the city.

The controller's job can be pivotal in the city's governance because of

charter provisions that give this person oversight over city activities. The controller is charged with ensuring that the city does not overspend. Under the charter, both the mayor and controller must sign all warrants or orders for payment before funds or moneys can be released from the city treasury. By refusing to sign, the controller can veto any expenditure of funds. This power is used more for obstructive purposes than as a veto. Thus, while the controller may refuse to authorize expenditures and the mayor and council lack formal authority to override him or her, in practice controllers have not used the power to stop specified expenditures entirely but rather to embarrass the mayor or to make a public statement by delaying payments.

Even when the controller uses this power, however, the mayor is not powerless. The mayor can use his or her executive position and influence to persuade the controller to agree to a proposed expenditure of funds. For example, the mayor can exert pressure by seeking a legal opinion from the city attorney. If the city attorney finds the expenditure legal and properly authorized, the controller is placed in a precarious position if he or she continues to oppose it.

Another potential source of the controller's negative power is his or her authority to estimate the ratio of total revenues and surpluses to expenditures. In the city's budgetary process, the mayor and council are required to balance proposed expenditures with the estimated total of revenues and surpluses, an estimate that is supplied and certified by the controller. By certifying a lower estimate, the controller can place the mayor in an embarrassing political position. The low estimate could cause a shortfall in revenues needed to meet service demands, with the mayor being the focal point for pressures arising from any service problem thus created.

Recently, an unprojected revenue shortfall in the city's municipal court system placed considerable pressure on the mayor's office and on the city's budgetary process. With a five-year low in the number of tickets issued by police officers, the city's municipal courts were experiencing monthly revenue shortfalls of greater than $2 million in the beginning of 1988. For some this indicated the revenue power that the police force can bring to bear on the mayor's office.

The city's civil service system is another institutional constraint on the mayor. Since 1913 city employees have been protected by a civil service system under rules that are currently established by a three-member citizen committee. Although the charter gives the mayor extensive authority to administer city business, practically all of the city's middle managers are outside the mayor's direct administrative control. Civil service protection is given to all city employees except department heads, some top managers

in the police and fire departments, city executives, selected executives and professionals in the legal department, and several less significant personnel. Civil service protection means that while the mayor can exercise policy direction and control at the top, he or she cannot ensure that second-level management will willingly implement city policy.

The Federal Presence

Since the beginning of the era of state-assisted oligopoly capitalism, the federal presence in Houston has evolved through three phases of development. Today, federal programs supporting services in all areas of life are found in Houston, and these programs are accepted by most as legitimate. This has not always been the case; for many years the federal presence in Houston was limited to specific types of programs. The expansion in federal assistance has altered local determination of priorities, but not solely because of direction from the federal government. Changes in the local environment have been important in determining the role of the federal government in the city. We have already described how the federal government has affected the Houston economy; in this section we examine its influence on politics.

Grass-Roots Federalism: 1930s–1940s

During the last century the federal government assisted states and localities in growth and development by supporting the development of the basic infrastructure of communities throughout the nation. In programs to open land for settlement, to make arid western land productive, to establish a canal system for drainage, flood control, and transportation, and to support the construction of schools, the emphasis was on "bricks and mortar" assistance. The federal government in effect subsidized the economic development of local communities without interference or direction. Programs were initiated and controlled at the grass-roots level.

From the very outset of community development in the last century—and continuing today—federal assistance was sought by both the public and private sectors in Houston when the need arose. As a result, local business and industrial efforts were directly subsidized by the federal government virtually without interference.

Generally speaking, federal assistance during the grass-roots era in Houston was specific to local community needs. The principal initiative

for assistance came from the private business sector—the local growth coalition—which sought support for its commercial-industrial endeavors. Federal aid in most cases was sought only after efforts to obtain local and state support were unsuccessful. While private entrepreneurs were eager to take advantage of aid, they were interested only in support for the goals they had defined. Indeed, enterprising local business interests even generated federal assistance for their projects when other governmental avenues at the local level failed. Thus, government and business leaders were practically indistinguishable in their goals. Local public officials were collaborators, partners in, and supporters of private initiatives for outside assistance. For the most part, there were no major disagreements about community priorities and federal assistance during the grass-roots era that supported those priorities and thus promoted local economic growth. When the creation of local units of government to administer federal projects became necessary, city and county officials dominated them by controlling their composition.

The development of the Houston ship channel is a good illustration of grass-roots federalism. Today, the Port of Houston and the ship channel are key factors in the area's economic success: along the channel are more than 150 enterprises that constitute a who's who of corporate giants.

From Houston's infancy, its merchants, commercial traders, and business leaders foresaw the advantages of a port linked to the Gulf of Mexico by a deep-water channel. They were convinced that such an improvement could be a key element in local economic growth, and thus in their own prosperity. By 1841 the Houston City Council had been persuaded to pass an ordinance creating a Port of Houston to facilitate ferry and commercial traffic southeast to Galveston along the Buffalo Bayou and southeast via the Brazos River. This modest beginning did not go far in promoting the use of the waterways, essentially because of their limited navigability. Therefore, local business interests sought financial assistance from both the city of Houston and the state of Texas to carry out improvements. Each responded with modest aid but nothing of the magnitude that would permit improvements on the scale envisioned.

Although their initial efforts were unsuccessful, the business leaders kept the concept of a deep-water channel and port in the forefront, first by organizing their own companies to do the actual work, and second by soliciting public support for their endeavors, initially from local sources and later from federal sources. In both cases, government and business worked in partnership—with the business leaders dominating the process. Business interests determined the priorities, and, even when disagreements

occurred, they were not over the ultimate objective—a port and deep-water channel—but only over the methods of attaining those ends.

In 1866 a group of private citizens formed the Houston District Navigation Company to instigate improvements in the bayou. The Houston City Council allied itself with the Navigation Company by appropriating $200,000 to speed its work and to sponsor a study of the feasibility of building a channel to the Gulf of Mexico. Then, in 1869, in anticipation of the study commission's findings, city business interests formed the Buffalo Ship Channel Company with the main goal of dredging a nine-foot channel to the Gulf of Mexico within three years. This company was to be directly supported by the city, since city funds and tolls would finance the project.[9]

Only after these privately generated endeavors fell short did the federal government become involved. In 1870 Houston was declared a port of entry, and a customshouse was authorized along with a survey of the bayou. Modest federal grants were obtained throughout the rest of the nineteenth century, but substantial federal assistance did not begin until around 1900. Then the federal involvement occurred because of the efforts of a coalition of local business leaders and state and local government officials. The coalition grew out of a relationship between the business leaders and area Congress members working together to obtain funds for channel improvements. Later, local officials aided in the creation of a local structure to finance and administer the improvement projects.

At the turn of the century a coalition of private business interests and public officials worked to ensure the success of ship-channel improvement projects. Mayor M. Baldwin Rice and U.S. Representative Thomas Ball succeeded in obtaining congressional approval for a local navigation district to supervise ship-channel improvement and to offer bonds to provide matching funds for federal dollars. After Congress approved their proposal in 1910, the voters of Harris County approved the creation of the Harris County Houston Ship Channel Navigation District and a $250,000 bond issue to support it. When the district failed to sell the bonds, Houston banks bailed it out.[10]

The Navigation District was the forerunner of the present-day Port of Houston Authority. The Houston City Council established a city harbor in 1913. Then, in 1922, the Navigation District and Harbor Board merged to form a five-member Port Commission. It is important to point out that the city of Houston and Harris County jointly determined the composition of the Port of Houston Authority. The mayor of Houston and the Harris County judge jointly nominate the chair of the commission.

Intergovernmental relations in the 1930s and 1940s were cooperative.

National, state, and local officials were in close contact. Furthermore, the federal government offered fiscal assistance to support state and local efforts in meeting wartime needs.[11]

Shortly after the outbreak of the war, executives of industries near or on the ship channel expressed dissatisfaction with their share of federal wartime contracts. With the support of area Congress members and local public officials, an intense lobbying effort was undertaken to persuade Washington to be more forthcoming with contracts.[12] The campaign resulted in massive federal expenditures for the purchase of fuels and explosives, cargo vessels and tankers, and a variety of other products from channel industries and for the provision of new plants to be constructed along the channel. By 1943 a total of 45 companies located on or near the channel had received $265 million in contracts from the federal government. "War contracts alone . . . increased by five times the number of industrial employees, the industrial payroll to ten times its normal size and the production of manufactured products in [the] city and county to a sum slightly less than four times its 1940 total."[13] By the end of the war over a billion federal dollars had filtered into the area's private economy. Business interests were satisfied with the federal support.

Federal wartime contracts to private industries laid the foundation for the multibillion-dollar industrial complex that now exists along the Houston ship channel. At the close of World War II the present petrochemical complex replaced wartime industries and grew to encompass what is now the "Golden Triangle" of Houston, Freeport, and Port Arthur.

Selected Advocacy, 1940s–1960s

Following World War II federal programs were focused on state and local problems revolving around postwar domestic needs. First, federal categorical grants proliferated to underwrite "much of the state-local effort to meet deferred wartime needs and also responded to changing technology and population configurations—especially that of suburbanization."[14] Second, federal programs came in response to middle-class service needs reinforcing the movement to the suburbs.

As the scope of federal involvement expanded, new patterns of intergovernmental relations emerged, but local officials had discretion in applying federal programs to local priorities. This degree of local control resembled that during the grass-roots era. The provision of most new federal programs allowed local officials to determine if they should be applied to their particular community problems. Initially, control and initiative re-

mained with the locality because its officials could choose those programs that met their community's special needs. But some localities became dependent on any and all federal aid. Others, like Houston, moved into the process more cautiously and selectively.

After World War II and into the 1960s, numerous federal programs helped growth and development in Houston. Although the programs differed from those of the grass-roots era in their content, compliance standards, and designated recipients, public and private leaders actively supported programs such as construction funds for airports and highways. A coalition of business, industrial, and government leaders was willing to comply with federal standards as long as federal dollars were filtered into capital-intensive projects. One of the most notable features of the selected-advocacy period was the ever-increasing involvement of the public sector. The types of federal assistance programs for state and local governments begun after World War II required more active involvement of elected and bureaucratic officials.[15] During the grass-roots period, local officials and state officials in the Houston metropolitan area operated mainly as conduits through which private business and industrial leaders' needs were transmitted to the national arena. Circumstances began to change in the selected-advocacy phase. Public officials became a more integral part of the federal aid process and not only took the lead in the advocacy process but were involved on a continuous basis because of the changed focus of federal programs. Public projects in housing, highways, sewage treatment plants, and airports required local officials to approve and administer them. Local officials became more distinct from their private-sector counterparts —if not in substantive concerns, then in form.

While local officials gained a measure of identity during the selected-advocacy era, they still supported the business interests in deciding what federal aid was needed. As had been true earlier, both public officials and business interests wanted federal programs that were capital-intensive and fostered economic growth and development. What had changed was that once a program was advocated, there were more conditions placed on the receipt of federal funds (e.g., building-height restrictions on approaches to airport runways, matching federal dollars, and rights-of-way for highways). As long as the program coincided with the business-government coalition's priorities for growth and development, the coalition was willing to comply with federal standards and conditions and even compromise local determination on certain measures. The important qualifier was that the change could not be too drastic or appear to alter the nature of growth and development. Thus the local coalition almost completely eschewed

federal programs, even if they were capital-intensive, that did not allow the private sector to choose what to build, where, when, and how, with minimal or no interference from government at any level. For example, programs were rejected if they dealt with inner-city deterioration and had social welfare components. Realtors, developers, business interests, and public officials rejected these programs because they were considered antagonistic to free-market endeavors.

Beginning in the late 1940s and through the mid-1960s, for example, Houston opposed public housing assistance and urban renewal at every turn.[16] Interestingly, the same members of the private sector who had beaten a path to Washington for wartime contracts and who strongly advocated federal funds for highway and airport construction were adamantly opposed to urban renewal. Houston's mayors and councils were in close accord with the business sector. As one city official explained, "Urban renewal was not even in our lexicon." [17] Not until 1960, when the council voted to accept a Mayor's Urban Redevelopment Committee recommendation to apply for a $60,000 HHFA (Housing and Home Finance Administration) urban renewal survey grant, did Houston even remotely entertain the idea of urban renewal. Even then, council approved the recommendation on a vote of five to three only after being assured that the survey would in no way obligate the city to attempt renewal or rehabilitation with federal funds.[18] For the growth coalition—the realtors, developers and other business interests that opposed urban renewal—the stakes were perceived to be too high. To them the conditions placed on the receipt of federal dollars far outweighed any benefits that might be derived from a renewal program. Along with local public officials, they had no desire to develop a program "for utilizing private and public resources"—a program that required approval of the administrator of HHFA and a local housing authority. To them it was a venture into socialism.[19]

But unlike urban renewal, federal funds to construct highways, airports, and flood-control projects suited the tastes of the growth coalition perfectly. Since World War II the Houston area has thrived on these programs. In 1952 alone, Houston received $235 million in federal highway assistance —53.7 percent of the total $435 million received by Texas that year.[20] A steady stream of federal dollars for flood control flowed into the area even before World War II, and federal construction money enabled Houston to build both Hobby Airport and the modern Intercontinental Airport.

No one in the private sector protested that these funds restricted local self-determination. Rather, local business leaders assisted in soliciting these funds and helped comply with conditions attached to their receipt. In

1957, for example, a prominent developer gave the city of Houston a ten-mile right-of-way for construction of the Southwest Freeway. Furthermore, while federal conditions on social programs were perceived as leading Houston down the path to socialism, those attached to urban and suburban development were viewed as merely doing business with the Feds.

The federal presence in Houston was both subtly and directly altered during the selected-advocacy phase. By accepting the conditions on programs for capital improvements, local officials legitimized the politics of the federal grant process. When local officials accepted conditions on federal dollars even when those dollars were used to meet local needs and priorities, local bargaining was placed in a different context than had been the case in the grass-roots era. Through city, county, and special district agencies, local officials were administering programs started and sometimes sustained by federal dollars. Houston created, for example, an aviation department and a housing authority, as well as community development and Comprehensive Employment and Training Act (CETA) departments. While control of these departments remained at the local level, federal ties developed. Significantly, a political relationship ensued, and federal input into the local decision-making process became increasingly acceptable. This input into economic growth programs already had legitimacy. Then, when the time came to move from advocating programs to fuel the local economy to advocating programs to address social maladies, the transition was facilitated by existing relationships established earlier when programs were accepted that had stimulated growth.

Drastic community changes also gave local officials cause to accept federal assistance for social programs. In the late 1960s and early 1970s local officials found themselves in a political vise between the business elite, which they appeared to want to support unequivocally, and a growing minority community whose voting strength was increasingly crucial in deciding elections. On the surface, the Houston area was the model of economic prosperity; yet throughout the area and particularly in the inner city, houses were deteriorating, as was the infrastructure of sewers, drainage facilities, and streets.

These problems were especially acute in minority neighborhoods; thus federal dollars were cost-effective not only economically but also politically. They allowed local officials to have the best of both worlds: programs to respond to a growing area that was moving at high speed outward to the suburbs and programs to reverse inner-city decay and stave off the increasingly volatile political problems associated with inner-city residents.

The Transition: Model Cities

A combination of factors moved Houston to advocate both types of federal assistance. While the transition occurred gradually and subtly, the watershed was the Model Cities program. In 1938 the Housing Authority of the City of Houston (HACH) was chartered as a nonprofit corporation, and subsequently made modest efforts to provide public housing assistance. In the 1960s, 2,190 units were built in four projects. Between 1950 and 1980 a total of 1,200 units in seven locations were added.[21] The simple fact is that throughout its 40-year history HACH has provided housing for only a miniscule portion of needy households. Not surprisingly, Houston ranks at the bottom in public housing assistance when compared with other large cities.[22]

Public housing was only minimally supported by city officials and at times vehemently opposed by realtors, developers, and business interests. In 1950, for example, HACH advocated federal assistance to build 2,500 housing units in blighted and slum areas. A referendum was called to decide the issue. Although Mayor Oscar Holcombe supported the proposal, it was defeated by a vocal opposition led by the real estate community, which attacked the plan as an intrusion by government planners on private home ownership.[23] While HACH is a nonprofit corporation, it does have ties to the city. The mayor of Houston appoints, with council approval, HACH's five commissioners. However, the city has chosen to let HACH fend for itself and has committed no funds to public housing.

In stark contrast to public housing, a Model Cities program for Houston brought Mayor Louis Welch support from leaders of various segments of the private sector. They campaigned hard for a grant by urging the adoption of a city housing code so that Houston would be in compliance with Model Cities regulations. As shown in Table 3.3, from 1966 to 1970 a series of events led up to the actual grant award.

During this period, pressures were increasing on local officials and their supporters from the community of realtors, developers, and business interests to do something about inner-city decay. As evidenced by findings of the Houston Council of Human Relations, the Mayor's Advisory Committee on Housing, and the U.S. Department of Justice, inner-city problems had reached a crisis level in the 1960s. This was true not only in the physical decay of the inner city but also in the discontent of the residents who lived in those areas. Mayor Welch perceived that the city had to deal with the emerging political power of the black community. Moreover, events outside the city influenced thinking in Houston. Widespread unrest was

Table 3.3   Major events in Houston's campaign for a Model Cities grant

Year	Event
1966	Houston Council of Human Relations (HCHR) conducted survey of 571 families who had been denied admission to public housing projects.
1967	HCHR issued report of survey findings. Recommended the adoption of a minimum housing code by the city of Houston.
	U.S. Department of Justice study found widespread dissatisfaction among Houston's blacks regarding employment, environment, and education.
	Mayor Louis Welch appointed a Citizens' Advisory Committee on Housing. Committee charged with identifying strategies for improving housing for the poor.
	HCHR issued second report; recommended that city of Houston seek Model Cities funding to deal with inner-city problems in minority communities.
	Housing Subcommittee of the Houston Chamber of Commerce urged Mayor's Advisory Committee to seek outside aid for local housing inadequacies.
	Mayor's Advisory Committee recommended to city that it apply for Model Cities funds.
1968	Houston City Council approved Model Cities grant application.
	City's application disapproved on the basis of no city housing code.
	Mayor Welch went to Washington to lobby for grant. After meeting with HUD and White House officials got promise of grant approval if Houston could attain approval of housing code.
1969	Welch and private leaders campaigned for housing code.
	Voters approved code.
1970	Model Cities grant approved.

occurring in black neighborhoods across the country. But the point to emphasize here is that socioeconomic and political factors within the Houston area appeared to be the primary reason for a changed attitude about advocating programs to deal with deterioration. While the availability of the Model Cities program helped, the solution was not imposed from the national level.

Once the coalition of local officials (led by Mayor Welch) and private leaders (led organizationally by the Houston Chamber of Commerce) became committed to the process of pursuing the federal grant, they did so unrelentingly. A housing code was acceptable to the mayor and private

leaders, and when Mayor Welch met opposition from the council he took the issue to the public. He was supported by civic groups and prominent business leaders. The coalition appeared to have decided that if it was necessary to pass a housing code to comply with federal regulations, then the coalition should retain control of the process as much as possible.

While the substantive impact of the Model Cities program is open to question, the impact on local political determination was lasting. By advocating the program for Houston, the coalition for the first time acknowledged the problem of housing deterioration publicly and pursued a solution through federal funding. In doing so, the coalition opened its own door—ever so narrowly—to segments of the minority community that had heretofore been totally excluded. This is not to say that the coalition extended membership—only that it acknowledged that minorities had become part of its calculations for the city's future.

Regulatory Federalism, 1970s–1980s

During the selected-advocacy era, aid was increased and less often controlled by local government and business interests. Both state and local officials were involved in the delivery of aid during this period. By the 1970s federal assistance had increased, and control became more concentrated in the hands of the federal and state governments.

The transformation in intergovernmental relations during the 1970s is most vividly illustrated in fiscal terms. As shown in Table 3.4, per capita federal aid and federal aid as a percentage of cities' own sources of revenue dramatically increased between 1972 and 1977. Fred Hofheinz, mayor from 1974 to 1978, opened the door both to more federal assistance and to Houston's poor and minority communities. George E. Hale and Marian Lief Palley summarize the general picture: "Local governments are increasingly turning to Washington to finance public buildings, roads, transit facilities, social services and salaries. In many jurisdictions a cutback in federal aid or even a slowdown in the growth rate of assistance can require drastic program cutbacks or major tax hikes. Large cities have become the most dependent on federal aid during recent years."[24] Federal aid became a fixture in many localities—including Houston—to support basic and essential services.

Houston and other major Texas cities are less dependent on federal aid than are other large cities, but Houston is not so different from other large cities in terms of the increase in the number of federal programs and in the amount of federal dollars in the city. Like other large cities, Texas cities

Table 3.4 Two measures of city dependency on federal aid: 1967, 1972, 1977

	Federal Aid[a]					
	Per capita (in dollars)			As a percentage of cities' own resources		
	1967	1972	1977	1967	1972	1977
All cities[b]	7.68	21.06	102.20	9.3	17.0	56.7
Texas[c]	2.13	6.06	55.56	6.0	10.0	49.0
Houston	2.25	3.01	34.55	4.0	4.0	21.0

[a]Federal aid, for cities, includes only direct receipts from the federal government. Indirect federal aid (state pass-throughs) is not appropriate to this analysis because these funds go almost entirely for welfare, highways, and education and thus go to special districts rather than cities.

[b]The 51 largest cities in the United States. Includes Texas cities.

[c]The 5 largest cities in Texas. Includes Houston.

Source: U.S. Department of Commerce, Bureau of the Census, *Classification Manual, Governmental Finances* (Washington, D.C.: U.S. Government Printing Office, 1976), p. 27.

generally and Houston particularly received increased direct federal aid per capita between 1967 and 1977. As shown in Table 3.4, per capita federal aid to Houston was 15 times greater in 1977 ($34.55) than in 1967 ($2.25). However, with the exception of San Antonio, Texas cities ranked lower than cities in other states in per capita federal aid between 1967 and 1977. With the exception of 1967, Houston ranked last among Texas cities in per capita federal aid (the 1967 anomaly is explained by airport construction funds received during that year) and, among the 51 largest cities in the United States, second from last in 1977 and sixth from last in 1972.[25]

Another measure of dependency is federal aid as a percentage of a city's own sources of revenue. Federal aid as a percentage of Houston's own sources of revenue was slightly over five times greater in 1977 (21 percent) than in 1967 (4 percent); however, it was more for other Texas cities and for cities outside Texas. Federal aid does not have the same significance in Houston as in other cities. Federal agencies cannot expect program dollars as compliance incentives to go as far in Houston as in cities that are more financially strapped. In addition, Houston's position at the bottom in both measures of dependency allows city officials to argue that Houston is not receiving its fair share of federal revenues. In both cases, the situation creates bargaining opportunities for local officials in the implementation of federal grants in Houston.

There was an enormous influx of federal dollars into Houston during the 1970s. Houston expended a total of $28.8 million in federal funds in 1973. By 1978 this amount had reached $211.7 million.[26] The rise in federal

dollars was accompanied by a rise in the number of federal programs, so that by the end of the 1970s the full array of federal acronyms dotted the ledger books at Houston's City Hall. Houston had CETA, CDBG, UMTA, and a number of others. An army of federal agencies was also involved with Houston in administering these programs.

The federal presence changed dramatically in a short period of time. The array of federal programs met both social and economic needs, and each type of assistance was welcomed by local officials. Instead of challenging the federal presence, Houston officials acknowledged that the federal government had a legitimate place in the city.

The Paradox of Local Control in Houston

While all types of federal aid are part of local calculations (i.e., local officials rely upon the assistance to underwrite the cost of essential services), there is still room for local control in how dollars are used and discretion in how the conditions affect the community. Paradoxically, local officials are given political latitude to manipulate grant conditions by the very factors that seem to lessen control. National programs may mandate that a local government undertake projects it might otherwise ignore or consider unimportant and endow the administering federal agency with authority to enforce compliance. But federal bureaucrats are often at the political mercy of local officials to implement program requirements, in large measure because of the same factors that appear to centralize control in Washington: grant proliferation, massive funding, uncertainty in program objectives, red tape, and the political ability of local officials to leverage their priorities in program implementation.[27]

In Houston, and in other communities as well, influence rests with that sector of the local community that can control local responses to federal grant conditions. The most influential segment of the Houston community has been the business sector allied with city leaders. The business sector has controlled economic growth programs while allowing others (blacks and Hispanics) to run federal social programs.

Private and public leaders who eschewed social programs during the initial years of the selected-advocacy era have been forced by political realities to accept these programs during the regulatory era. Since 1973 blacks, Hispanics, and interest groups traditionally allied with minorities (e.g., organized labor) have become a more powerful coalition in each

succeeding citywide election. Successful mayoral candidates, beginning with Fred Hofheinz in 1973, have had to incorporate minorities in their election strategy and to combine that support with the traditional backing of the business community, especially developers and realtors. The growth of minority influence at the polls was also matched by the growth of federal funds to support programs that most affected the quality of life in inner-city minority neighborhoods. As a result, minority communities have had an important role in the development and administration of the federal programs.[28]

As an example of this growth of minority influence, after taking office Mayor Whitmire hired a Hispanic, Efraim Garcia, to head the city's planning and development department, which oversees the city's use of its multimillion-dollar Community Development federal funds.[29] However, and perhaps related to the city's lack of experience with federal Community Development moneys, Garcia's resignation was accepted by the mayor in 1988 after federal auditors estimated that the city would lose over $2 million in federal funds that would not be spent by the end of the fiscal year. Previously, in 1986, the city returned $1.2 million in Community Development funds because the city did not spend the funds fast enough.

The traditionally powerful business sector and its allies among Houston mayors, city department heads, and most members of the city council have generally endorsed federally funded social programs and those that deal with inner-city decay as minority plums to be administered by minorities. Thus, administrative offices for programs such as CETA and Community Development were established in the mayor's office, and these programs were administered by representatives of the minority community, particularly blacks.[30]

On the other hand, federal programs that aid development and that most affect business interests are integrated into traditional city departments. As MacManus maintains:

Business and industrial groups have played an important part in deciding how funds will be spent from revenue sharing, local public works, UMTA, and EPA grants. The push by the Houston Chamber of Commerce for continued economic development as well as revitalization of deteriorating inner-city neighborhoods has prompted the city to solicit grants for these purposes. Priorities within these programs have been largely the responsibility of the appropriate city department heads, who often receive advice from the business leaders.[31]

Thus, through the 1970s the Houston business community with the co-operation of city officials has generally let minorities use the federal social programs as they think appropriate, while the business community has taken care of the federal programs that most affect growth and development and business profits. This approach to federal-program administration has opened one segment of city government to minority participation, at least to some minority leaders. Symbolically, it has been important in recognizing black and brown political strength in elections and city policy. The limited participation of minorities in social programs has, however, allowed the business community to continue its control of growth and development in Houston.

Summary

A number of changes in the characteristics of local determination have occurred in the pursuit and implementation of federal programs in the era of state-assisted oligopoly capitalism. For instance, internal pressure for change has largely replaced external efforts to impose it. As detailed above, for example, in local administration of federal programs there has been increased participation of minorities. Also, local structures have been expanded and altered to respond to inner-city as well as growth problems. And there has been a marriage of convenience between the traditionally powerful business sector and minorities. The incentives for this marriage have been federal programs that both sides have wanted. While there has been considerable change in how local priorities are determined both in the public and private sectors, the political, social, and economic circumstances within the community distinctly influence the use of federal assistance.

4

Neighborhood Groups
and Development:
A Question of Participation and Elites

While Chapters 2 and 3 illustrate the dominant role of Houston's growth coalition and business, development, and political leaders in directing the nature of development, a variety of neighborhood groups seek to have some influence over the nature of growth. In this chapter we broaden our focus on Houston's growth by examining various types of community-based groups and their role in affecting Houston's growth. In this chapter we further illustrate Houston's social mosaic through our examination of the efforts of community, neighborhood, and other citizens' groups to influence land use in Houston.

One distinctive feature of Houston's history is the relative lack of struggle over neighborhood change and redevelopment. One reason for the absence of recent community protest may be the character of Houston's development. In many U.S. cities since the 1960s, community protests, including ghetto riots, centered on the destructive effects of development and redevelopment programs. As we noted in Chapters 2 and 3, Houston has seen no publicly subsidized urban renewal programs and, since much of the city has been built since the 1950s, there has been little redevelopment by private developers. While scattered, small-pocket gentrification has occurred, no large communities have been displaced by public or private redevelopment since the 1960s. One office building may occasionally replace another, and a few large-scale projects like Greenway Plaza may displace 300 families, but these are rare and the areas displaced generally have not been areas with neighborhood organizations strong enough to mount significant resistance. Indeed, in the Greenway Plaza case there was *no* organized protest of any kind from the displaced families in four residential subdivisions.

There has been community organization in Houston, yet it typically is

of a distinctive, low-protest type, such as civic clubs. Historically, portions of a few minority areas have been partially displaced by highway construction, as in the case of two highway projects in the black Fifth Ward during the 1950s. But the racial repression in Houston prior to the 1970s —for example, a police department with a reputation as the most brutal in the nation—kept minority communities from organizing any significant resistance to the limited types of displacement that have occurred. While the rising voting strength of minorities has begun to alter this picture, this conflict is just beginning to be evident in Houston in the 1980s. By the standards of most other cities there is little overt neighborhood conflict between Houston's minority and white working-class communities and its white business-political establishment. Even during the peak of the civil rights movement in the 1960s, Houston saw much less protest than elsewhere (see Chapters 5 and 6 for details). In this chapter we seek to explain the modest level of citizen organization in Houston.[1]

The Context of Community Organization:
The Free-Market Ideology and the
Business Growth Coalition

As we have noted several times previously, Houston is a city in which the dominant ideology is that of the free market, in the sense that the local government supposedly takes a hands-off approach to private development. Houston has few government restrictions on development, and it is a tax haven for individuals and businesses. In addition to the characterization of Houston as a city (allegedly) free from federal and state government interference, the emphasis is on a relatively weak local government aligned with local business interests. Illustrative of this laissez-faire ideology is the following excerpt from a 1980 guidebook on Houston:

> Much of the city's growth can be attributed to the local government's attitude of cooperation with the business community. Houston is the major city with the least amount of regulations and restrictions. Perhaps the key element in Houston's continually growing and historically sound economy has been a consistently positive attitude towards the free enterprise system. This desirable business climate has stimulated the expansion of economic activities.[2]

While the accuracy of the image of Houston as a free enterprise city is questionable, the effects of this ideology on the nature of resistance to

development cannot be ignored in the examination of neighborhood and citizen responses to business and industrial expansion in Houston.[3]

As early as the 1860s Houston had a growth coalition of local merchants and other entrepreneurs who worked to develop the city. Platt noted that Houston's "prominent entrepreneurs and its city manager were virtually one and the same . . . and this . . . guaranteed a large overlap in the interests and outlook of the public and private sectors."[4] Private and public cooperation and collaboration on projects were the dominant forms of development during the nineteenth century.[5] During the early twentieth century Houston grew at a fast pace, with growth exceeding 30 percent in every decade (Chapter 2). Major industry moved into Houston and the Sunbelt by the early decades of the twentieth century. Some of this development was fostered by the growing infrastructure supporting urban development. The widening and deepening of the Houston ship channel, the development of a port facility, and expanded sewer and water systems contributed to the development of Houston as an industrial center.

Concurrent with the development of the necessary infrastructure, Houston announced its availability as a center for outside investors. In spite of the efforts of Houston's growth coalition to provide the necessary infrastructure services and of efforts to project an image of Houston as a center for industry, Houston remained a small city until its rapid growth in the post–World War II era. During World War II significant amounts of capital were channeled into the Houston economy. War Production Board expenditures increased the local physical plant significantly.[6] Petrochemical research and production increased during World War II and contributed to the postwar profitability of the petrochemical industry.[7]

After the war Houston began a long economic boom fueled by the rising national demand for oil and oil products. Earlier state and federal aid in the oil and petrochemical industry placed Houston and its industries in an advantageous position to benefit from the postwar boom. During this period the Texas coastal area became a major location for investors from outside the state. The oil and petrochemical economy generated investment from related industries, and at the same time shipping and other related industries moved into the area. In the early 1960s Lyndon Johnson succeeded in attracting NASA to the Houston area.[8]

Residential Expansion and the
Growth of Civic Associations

In discussing the growth of the business community and the expansion of commercial and industrial areas in Houston, we must examine the devel-

opment of residential communities and neighborhoods in the city. In the post–World War II growth spurt, several developments occurred simultaneously. Houston's rapidly expanding population led to the creation of new neighborhoods, and intensified efforts to maintain ethnic homogeneity in both the existing and new neighborhoods and communities. In addition, many neighborhoods also tried to safeguard their communities from commercial and industrial development—a difficult task given the absence of zoning in Houston.

It was in this post–World War II period that most civic clubs in Houston were formed. Given the absence of zoning, developers would typically file deeds containing restrictions on the possible uses of the property. Once deed restrictions were filed with the legal department, the responsibility of reporting violations rested with developers, individual citizens, or civic clubs. During the early stages of development in an area, the developer normally acted as the primary watchdog for deed restriction violations. Once most of the property in an area was sold, the responsibility for deed restriction enforcement fell to individual residents. In an effort to efficiently monitor deed restriction enforcement, civic clubs were formed during this period of rapid growth.

During the 1940s and 1950s private deed restriction enforcement maintained the character of neighborhoods; yet there were limits to the effectiveness of private enforcement. The first steps in the enforcement process involved informal measures taken to notify the offender of the violation of a deed restriction.[9] While in many cases informal enforcement was successful, sometimes more formal actions were required. Formal actions that could be taken by civic associations included civil lawsuits, or the threat of civil lawsuits.[10] The expense of civil lawsuits precluded any but the most affluent areas from taking this action to enforce deed restrictions.

In addition to the enforcement of building restrictions, civic clubs attempted to maintain racial homogeneity within their neighborhoods (cf. Chapter 5). After 1948, when the legal exclusion of blacks from white areas was no longer possible, informal efforts to maintain neighborhood homogeneity were intensified. Neighborhood stabilization efforts in the 1950s and 1960s were primary concerns of civic associations. After the 1948 *Shelly* decision, neighborhood associations sought to preserve the racial homogeneity of their areas through such efforts. The Allied Civic Clubs (ACC) was one organization formed to deal with the issue of neighborhood integration. Acting as an umbrella organization for neighborhood associations in southwest Houston, the ACC sought to stop the complete racial transformation of neighborhoods.[11] One tactic to forestall neighbor-

hood integration was to encourage white homeowners to beware of realtors willing to sell houses to black families. By such action the ACC argued that all-white areas would have a much better chance of remaining all-white. Other civic associations also focused on the "problem" of racial integration, especially in the 1950s.

During the 1950s neighborhood transition occurred despite neighborhood stabilization efforts, so that many predominantly white areas became predominantly black, and whites moved to outer-city locations. With Houston's liberal annexation policy, few of these new white areas remained outside the city but were annexed.[12] The greater distance between white residential areas and black residential areas lessened the pressure to maintain racially segregated communities, and civic associations began to focus on neighborhood enhancement. The Southwest Civic Club (SWCC), for example, was organized to acquire services from the city or to provide those services. As such, its focus was on deed restriction enforcement and mosquito fogging more than on maintaining racial segregation. Of course, the SWCC was in an affluent area geographically removed from the minority communities of Houston.

Civic associations are mostly located in white areas and act to maintain control of commercial development near residential neighborhoods. As outlined above, the most affluent civic associations are most effective in maintaining full enforcement of deed restrictions. Civic associations also seek to limit commercial development in and near their neighborhoods even when there are no deed restrictions prohibiting such development. A development may be stopped if it can be shown that it will produce traffic congestion or water problems (through runoff or contamination of water supplies, for example). Some civic associations have used this tactic to forestall commercial development, since it is virtually their only weapon in the absence of deed restrictions and zoning. In this sense, civic associations serve a land-use function not dissimilar to zoning.[13]

In addition to the maintenance of racially segregated neighborhoods and the limitation of commercial development, civic associations are concerned with the delivery of city services. Civic associations focus much of their efforts on obtaining mosquito fogging, streetlights, and sidewalks in their neighborhoods. Although the civic associations see themselves as nonpolitical, they have played a political role by influencing local officials on behalf of their neighborhoods and by emphasizing local—that is, neighborhood—territorial control.[14] In this sense the actions of community-based organizations are not in conflict with the sentiments of former mayor Louis Welch. Welch, a local developer, was quoted as saying that Hous-

ton did not need parks because people had backyards; community-based groups seek to improve their own "backyards."

Along with the territorial-control functions of civic associations, "cultural identity" goals can also be found within many civic associations.[15] Members of many associations perceive that city and state governments are not interested either in the maintenance of stable neighborhoods or in the delivery of services.[16] In these organizations there is an effort to develop community cohesiveness and stability, ensure local control over the delivery of services, and meet resident and neighborhood needs. Civic associations make proposals for specific city services that the neighborhood residents themselves define as necessary, rather than letting the city decide on appropriate services.

The multiple purposes and goals of neighborhood civic associations in Houston may partially account for their relative longevity and strength. This stability is in contrast to the relative weakness of more progressive neighborhood associations in Houston.[17]

Civic associations, as a group, have had an impact on development in part because they have been in existence for a long period of time. Much of the impact of civic associations has been in limiting the type of nonresidential development in residential areas through enforcement of deed restrictions. A second area of some impact is in the delivery of social services; civic associations have been successful in securing such services from the city as streetlights, mosquito fogging, and park development.

Neighborhood Organizations and the Poor

Neighborhood organizations, similar in many respects to the traditional civic clubs, also are active in Houston.[18] Recently, neighborhood-based organizations in areas where community groups are less common have been formed through the efforts of the Neighborhood Revitalization Office of the City of Houston Planning Department, and The Metropolitan Organization (TMO). A modest number of neighborhood organizations have arisen in predominantly low- or moderate-income and minority areas.[19] While the efforts of these organizations are often centered primarily on neighborhood maintenance, the specific goals of these groups are not identical to those of the traditional civic associations. The poor and minority organizations formed through alliance with TMO are different in approach from those participating through the Neighborhood Revitalization Office of the City of Houston Planning Department. Neighborhood organizations affiliated with the Neighborhood Revitalization Office are more like

civic associations in tactics and goals than are TMO organizations. Rather than focusing on gaining power to make decisions about their neighborhoods directly, organizations affiliated with the Neighborhood Revitalization Office make efforts to represent their interests to the city in order to facilitate the revitalization and maintenance of their neighborhoods. The majority of neighborhood associations affiliated with the Neighborhood Revitalization Office focus almost exclusively on "collective consumption" goals, such as the provision of mosquito fogging, streetlights, and even some public-private commercial developments. El Mercado, a commercial development in east Houston, is an example of an effort supported by the neighborhood organization but basically built by private developers in conjunction with the city of Houston. Located in a low- and moderate-income sector, the project was designed to stimulate redevelopment in the area. Although El Mercado was touted as a source of new jobs as well as new business opportunities, it failed and has been rescued from foreclosure by the city (at least temporarily).

TMO organizes through existing community (e.g., Catholic church) leaders and organizations to effect change.[20] TMO-affiliated organizations focus on the delivery of services and on collective-consumption issues, as well as on gaining power and fighting problems associated with powerlessness.[21] TMO was founded in Houston in 1979 and currently has approximately 65 churches and neighborhood organizations affiliated with it. It concentrates on training leaders within communities, usually within churches in the communities, to lead area citizens' movements. An example of a TMO effort similar to those of traditional civic associations is its recently successful push to get Houston bond money committed to improve lights and roads and to build libraries in the low- and moderate-income areas where TMO has organized.[22] TMO concentrates on winning concrete gains as well as on empowering citizens of participant neighborhoods, but little emphasis is placed on large-scale social change. In this way TMO is similar to traditional civic associations; it is a territorial organization and focuses primarily on quality-of-life issues.[23] Political power is seen mainly as a means of meeting collective-consumption goals.

Until recently, ACORN was active in Houston. For several years ACORN organizations in Houston worked to establish legal channels for homesteading. Homesteading is the physical occupation of a house that has been unoccupied and delinquent in taxes for a significant period of time. Until ACORN efforts there was little official support for homesteading. Yet through the efforts of organizations associated with ACORN, two city council members in Houston pledged to help establish means for

legal homesteading. This was a significant success for neighborhood organizations, especially those in predominantly minority areas with a large
number of neglected homes.[24]

In addition to working toward establishment of legal channels for homesteading, community organizations affiliated with ACORN focused on
community control in another way—through the issue of police protection.
Neighborhood organizations in Houston's Third Ward, a predominantly
black, low-income area, have successfully collaborated with the Houston
Police Department to have police personnel who themselves reside in the
Third Ward work in the area. This effort was designed to produce better police/citizen communication and better police service in the area. By
having police officers familiar with the neighborhoods to which they are
assigned, better police service is achieved, according to Judy Graves of
ACORN.[25]

Neighborhood-based grass-roots movements affiliated with ACORN
targeted other issues for remedial action, including the maintenance of a
subsidized housing project and the support of neighborhood schools in
low-income areas.[26] In the effort to maintain Allen Parkway Village, a public housing project scheduled for demolition, an ACORN-affiliated group
tried to prevent the Houston Housing Authority from selling the property.
According to Graves, the Houston Housing Authority neglected repairs at
Allen Parkway Village, a project located near downtown Houson on desirable commercial land. After years of this neglect, the Houston Housing
Authority got approval from the federal government to sell the property.
Residents organized to try to block the sale of the project.

ACORN-affiliated groups made attempts to keep open schools that were
targeted for closing, usually in primarily black areas. In May 1984 the
school board agreed to keep open three schools for at least two years. The
ultimate goal is permanently to prevent the closing of the schools.[27]

While TMO and the neighborhood organizations affiliated with the
Neighborhood Revitalization Office are not nearly as strong as the more
traditional (and predominantly white) civic associations, they have brought
some organization to Houston's poor and minority communities in recent
years. The TMO- and ACORN-affiliated groups have addressed a broader
range of issues than the civic clubs; but the effectiveness of these groups'
efforts is unclear. Their modest power may have something to do with citizen fatalism about the costs and problems associated with urban growth.
At the very least, these militant neighborhood-based groups provide the
potential for expanded citizen protest in the future.

More recently formed neighborhood organizations in low- and moderate-income and minority areas are pursuing many of the goals pursued by older civic associations. These neighborhood organizations have secured streetlights, sidewalks, and vacant lot cleanups, as well as more significant infrastructure services. The city services secured by neighborhood organizations and civic associations challenge the image of Houston as only a center for profit; services of a specific type and quality are demanded by citizens organized into community-based movements.

Environmental Organizations

Environmental organizations in Houston, while generally weak and episodic in formation, are nevertheless significant enough to warrant attention. Environmental groups most often form in response to serious environmental problems, though there is relatively little prolonged action by stable organizations.

Citizens' groups have organized in response to environmental pollution near Pasadena. A small Pasadena citizens' group formed after the U.S. Steel Chemical Company burned off a large amount of ethylene in 1983. The burnoff produced ill effects in residents near the plant. After the violation of air-quality standards by the company, 2 notices of violation were issued, adding to the 35 notices the company had previously received between 1978 and 1983.[28] The citizens' group formed only after a burnoff that immediately adversely affected the citizens in the area.

A second citizens' reaction to a specific event occurred in 1980, when Stauffer Chemical spewed gas into a southeast Houston neighborhood. TMO handled negotiations for the citizens in the area and secured an agreement from Stauffer Chemical to pay the medical costs of individuals requiring treatment after the incident. An alarm and evacuation system was also installed by Stauffer.[29]

The Citizens' Environmental Coalition, an umbrella organization providing information to community-based organizations, is the major environmental-action group in Houston. The limited impact of environmental groups in Houston is primarily a result of their small size, episodic nature, and lack of sustained action. They have, however, managed to affect the operation of some petrochemical companies at least minimally as well as to bring attention to the issue of environmental pollution.

Environmental groups' goals are a mixture of collective-consumption and political-power goals. Political power is sought in order to gain control

over the neighborhoods and the chemical contamination of those neighborhoods. Collective-consumption goals are manifested in the pressure for improved city services, including environmental cleanup.

While not as numerous or strong as civic organizations, environmental groups have addressed somewhat larger issues well beyond single neighborhoods. The issues raised by various environmental groups challenge some assumptions regarding environmental responsibilities made by businesses, specifically those in the petrochemical industry. Environmental-action organizations have in several instances forced polluters to pay for some of the consequences of their pollution, including medical costs incurred by residents affected by pollutants. In spite of the broader demands made by environmental groups, their overall impact on industrial pollution has been minimal so far. Primarily reacting to crisis situations, they have made little sustained effort at changing the practices of polluting industries.

Business Organizations: The Real Power Brokers

Rapid unplanned growth as well as the recent economic downturn in Houston resulted in a proliferation of organizations representing business, development, and corporate interests. Like civic and neighborhood associations, these business associations are chartered to respond to and affect patterns of development in Houston. Although listed as community groups by the City of Houston Department of Planning and Development, these organizations are very different from traditional civic and neighborhood associations. The quality-of-life issues these business associations address are tied directly to the business climate of Houston and as such are different from the quality-of-life concerns of civic associations. These business associations operate to ensure that Houston remains attractive as a location for corporate headquarters and development.[30]

One of the social costs of growth that most business associations address is transportation and traffic congestion. Troubled by Houston's reputation for traffic congestion, business associations deal with both the problem and the image of the problem. During the early 1980s several business associations put forward proposals to the Metropolitan Transit Authority, the State Highway Department, and the city of Houston to deal with traffic flow in high-growth areas of Houston. The major interest of business groups is to ensure accessibility, both now and in the future. The West Houston Association, a group of corporations, developers, and other business interests, was founded in 1978 to meet the three basic goals of providing a comprehensive transportation system, providing a full range of urban

services, and enhancing and protecting the environment.[31] To distinguish these goals from the goals of civic and neighborhood associations, a closer examination is necessary. Stofer provides the following information:

> The West Houston Association was founded in 1978 by . . . corporate executives and real estate developers who were concerned that unrestrained growth occurring in the absence of planning and coordination might negatively affect the high quality of life that first attracted them to the area.[32]

The West Houston Association represents the interests of corporations and developers in the far western part of the city. This "energy corridor" is one of the fastest-growing areas in terms of population and jobs. Between 1983 and 1984 the area's population grew by 9 percent, with employment increasing by 11,000 jobs.[33] Only recently have real estate associations been willing to accept planning and coordination, activities formerly considered as part of an anti-free-enterprise philosophy by Houston's business elite.

City Post Oak Association (CPOA) is composed of business interests and represents the Galleria/Post Oak area, a major retail and office center area also west of downtown. Formed in 1976, CPOA, like the West Houston Association, concentrates much of its attention on traffic improvements.[34] CPOA-sponsored traffic improvements include the institution of van pooling, street improvements, and bus stop shelters.[35] Proposals for highway improvements have been made to the State Department of Highways and Public Transportation and to the Houston Traffic and Transportation Department. Business and developer associations are more likely to work closely with local government officials than are civic and neighborhood associations, since they often share the same economic backgrounds as the officials. In addition to proposing improvements, business associations fund some improvements and as such offer material incentives for city and state government collaboration. Area business associations are among the strongest "independent" organizations in Houston and work closely with other central business associations (e.g., the Houston Chamber of Commerce).

A second type of business-oriented organization in Houston is the image-building association. One such association was *Pro-Houston,* a "cheerleading" association designed to "rekindle the 'can-do' spirit in the city." [36] Composed of business and community leaders, *Pro-Houston* was a campaign designed to improve the *image* of Houston, an image tarnished

by media recognition of the social costs of growth in the city.[37] The image building was designed to maintain Houston's position as a prime location for business and corporate profit making.

Houston's current image-building campaign is called "Houston Proud" and is similar to the "Miami Nice" campaign. Once again, this campaign is designed to change the image of the city rather than to alleviate concrete problems.

Like civic associations, business organizations have been successful in achieving their major goals of securing infrastructure services, such as road building, from the city. Furthermore, they, like civic associations, also focus on the delivery of services provided by the city. Unlike civic associations, however, business organizations are interested in securing services that will support continued development. Business organizations, particularly the territorial business associations, are in many instances located in areas contiguous to residential areas with strong civic associations.

Conflicts among Community and Business Associations

The disparate interests of progressive community-based movements and business organizations are well illustrated by a Houston Chamber of Commerce Action Plan. In a 1980–1981 Action Plan, the Houston Chamber of Commerce warned of impending strains on the delivery of city services. The chamber recognized the formation of neighborhood-based citizens' associations and the possibility for challenges to the business elite. It stated its concerns over the impact of rapid growth in the 1980–1981 Action Plan: "Houston's people problems will become felt increasingly by the entire community. Militant radicals will become more of a problem, as they attempt to establish leadership roles with largely uneducated and unsophisticated groups." [38] The existence of conflict over the development of Houston is clear. The formation of progressive citizens' associations potentially unfriendly to chamber of commerce and business interests was viewed as a significant problem as early as 1980. The 1980–1981 Action Plan goes on to call for the "support of creditable leaders" among the various citizens' groups. Moreover, the chamber of commerce sees itself as the organization best suited to provide the leadership and coordination among interest groups in Houston.

Interestingly, the Houston Chamber of Commerce Action Plan calls for citizens' groups to focus on neighborhood improvement and maintenance, including the upkeep of parks and recreational areas. These activities supported by the chamber of commerce are basically the same as those pursued

by traditional civic associations. In this instance, the goal of the leading business association is the co-optation and control of progressive, non-business-oriented neighborhood associations. The chamber sees citizen involvement as good if it is focused on the nondisruptive goals of neighborhoods. Even the development of a sense of community pride is seen as good for business as long as it focuses on issues that do not threaten continued growth.

Conflict among business organizations and progressive neighborhood organizations, property owners, or civic associations is also illustrated by conflicting ideas about the future of the Fourth Ward. The Fourth Ward is one of Houston's oldest black communities, located between the Central Business District and River Oaks, the most prestigious residential area in Houston. The location of the Fourth Ward on prime real estate has created a conflict over the future development, or redevelopment, of the area.

Central Houston Incorporated, a business organization for "the betterment of downtown," is a major organization supporting the commercial and residential development of the Fourth Ward. In an effort to bring middle- and upper-income housing near downtown, Central Houston Incorporated has proposed the black Fourth Ward community as a possible site for major redevelopment, with substantial public-sector involvement. Given the price of land in the Fourth Ward (approximately $20 per square foot), the cost of new housing in this area after redevelopment would be well above the rent of $100 per month paid by many current residents.[39]

Freedman's Town Association, the black neighborhood organization in the Fourth Ward representing current residents, is resisting the efforts of business interests to redevelop the area. The efforts of Freedman's Town Association involve support for historical-district status for some sections of the Fourth Ward. The seeking of such status is a reaction to redevelopment efforts by private developers and the City of Houston Department of Planning and Development.[40] The Allen Parkway Village Residents' Council has been working to preserve Allen Parkway Village (APV), a low-income housing project located in the Fourth Ward and one of the largest public housing projects in Houston. Beginning in 1977 private developers approached the Housing Authority of the City of Houston (HACH) to purchase the land on which APV sits. In July 1984, the Houston City Council approved plans to demolish APV. The recent decision to demolish APV culminates a seven-year effort by developers to acquire the APV land. HACH has purposely let APV deteriorate in order to justify the decision to demolish the project.[41]

In spite of the partial successes of HACH, of business interests, and of

developers in the Fourth Ward, the efforts of neighborhood-based organizations have made the fate of the Fourth Ward and APV a public, controversial issue. The business interests, often supported by city government, prevail in conflicts over the form of development more often than do tenants' and neighborhood-based organizations; yet the public nature of some of these recent battles illustrates the delegitimizing role that community-based groups may play. That is, the definition of the city simply as a place to make a profit is challenged.

Conceptualizing Local Urban Conflict   The conflict over the future of the Fourth Ward points up the disparate interests involved in debates over the nature of future development in Houston. Freedman's Town Association and Allen Parkway Village Residents' Association are groups focused on a variety of goals that are not directly related to the production of profit. The progressive organizations in the Fourth Ward are demanding services from the city, the right to determine the future of their neighborhood, and the recognition and preservation of the history of the Fourth Ward. Much of the effort by organizations within the Fourth Ward is to acquire and gain control over the provision of city support services for the neighborhood and to replace or avoid external control over the area.

At the same time, property owners' associations, developers, and the City of Houston Department of Planning and Development are striving to acquire and maintain control over the Fourth Ward. These groups are seeking to define the city, with the Fourth Ward as one example, as a center for the production and maximization of profit. They are united in denying the legitimacy of neighborhood maintenance in and of itself, the provision of city services, and local neighborhood (community) control as important elements to maintain in communities and neighborhoods. The Fourth Ward conflict provides a dynamic example of these competing interests.

Rather than trying to conceptualize these conflicts within the city in terms of a two-class (capitalists/workers) model of conflict, it is more useful to view them as revolving around a variety of interests.[42] Saunders's argument that a two-class model of production-class interests is most appropriate at the level of national social investment policies, with more diverse race and class interests involved in decision making and social consumption expenditures at the local level, fits the reality of conflicting interests in Houston.

As noted previously, this two-pronged approach, with national-level and local-level decision making conceptualized differently, requires a recognition of classes or interests formed somewhat separately from the production process. In addition, such an approach necessitates a view of these interests

as something other than distortions of "real" class (i.e., production-class) interests.[43] The definition of interests at the local level as representing consumption-sector interests is a useful method for incorporating analyses of local politics into larger political-economic analyses. At the level of local interests, group or class affiliation may arise from similarities in consumption patterns (e.g., property ownership, tenant status). A major force supporting the formation and stability of neighborhood associations are the common interests resulting from inhabiting a common area: the neighborhood.[44]

In order for analyses of community movements to be integrated into a larger model of class interests, consumption-sector interests must be recognized and used as the basis for analyzing the activities of community-based movements. The community-based movements in Houston are, for the most part, based on common consumption interests. Moreover, these consumption-sector interests have produced somewhat more powerful movements than those organizations based on production-class interests—unions, for example—although their conflict is primarily with business organizations that are basically production-class interest groups.

Summary of the Impact of Community-Based Movements

The activities of community-based movements in Houston have not fundamentally altered the definition of the city as a location for the production of exchange values (profit), but some changes have occurred. The services provided by the city government, collective-consumption provisions, are more equally distributed, and the services to be delivered are more often determined by residents of the areas in question (as opposed to outside sources). The recent efforts of business organizations, on the other hand, represent a trend in Houston—business lobbying the city government for infrastructure services. Generally, Houston is characterized as a city in which the city government "naturally" operates in the interests of business, but this perception is not supported in light of the lobbying efforts of business interests. The business organizations have been successful in spurring infrastructure development by the city to support further growth and development. While communities have been able to extract services and goods from the city, as well as from private industry, the business organizations active in Houston politics are generally more successful in acquiring commitments from the city government than are community organizations. We now turn to Houston's black (Chapter 5) and Hispanic (Chapter 6) communities.

5

Patterns of Racial and Ethnic
Disparity and Conflict:
The Black Community

Houston's black and Hispanic communities are important in an examination of Houston's growth because they include many of the low-wage workers who built the city. We have noted the importance of national and multinational firms in the city's emergence as a major metropolitan center, but we have just touched on the labor inputs to that growth and the uneven, often negative, effects of economic growth and decline on minority Houstonians. These men and women have played a central role in the construction of the city. The growth machine in Houston has run primarily on the energy of its human population, including its minority enclaves. From the slave labor of the mid-nineteenth century to the more recent undocumented ("illegal") Mexican and Central American immigrants, the city's large black and Hispanic labor pools provided much of the unskilled labor that constructed bridges, water systems, factories, railroads, highways, office buildings, and houses. Stereotyped, discriminated against, exploited, and abused, black and Hispanic workers have done much of the daily construction, especially the "dirty work," that has built Houston. The image of independence, prosperity, and glitter often associated with the city's growth has obscured not only a basic dependence on outside corporations and governmental aid but also the substantial dependence on these cohorts of workers.

The seamy side of Houston can be seen in the lives of its minority residents, who have not done nearly as well as white entrepreneurs and white workers over the last few decades. While it was argued in the early 1980s that the boom in Sunbelt cities benefited everyone and that poverty in the same cities became insignificant, this is problematic. The 1950s–1970s boom in Houston did keep unemployment down, but it brought jobs at *low* wages for many of Houston's working people—and especially for its black and brown working people. Typically, for large sectors of

the population wages have been very low and prosperity has not meant a significant reduction in the discrimination faced by minority citizens. Discrimination remains an impediment to employment, housing, and education equality for Houston's black and Hispanic citizens. Prosperity for some white Houstonians has meant little advance for minority Houstonians, who have had to cope with decades of racial discrimination and neglect. Moreover, Houston's recent economic decline, while hurting the white community, has meant an even sharper socioeconomic deterioration for its minority residents.

Historical Antecedents: Blacks in Houston's Past

The presence of black workers and their families dates back to Houston's beginning as a mosquito-infested swampland. The original town site was cleared by black slaves and Mexican laborers, for it was feared that "no white man could have worked and endured the insect bites and malaria, snake bites, impure water, and other hardships." [1] The early Houston economy was centered around cotton and sugar production. The city's black slaves worked largely as domestic servants; black laborers also worked in the trades and on the wharves. [2]

Houston's black slave population remained relatively small until the 1860s. On Emancipation Day in Texas (June 19, 1865, or "Juneteenth"), there were approximately 1,000 blacks in Houston. However, after Juneteenth a steady stream of newly freed slaves began migrating to Houston to fill the growing demand for labor. By 1900, at the start of its era of competitive-industrial capitalism, the city's 14,608 blacks constituted nearly one-third of the city's total population of 44,633. Former slaves settled in a section of the city's Fourth Ward that later became known as "Freedman's Town." Freedman's Town and the surrounding Fourth Ward became a thriving center for black business and commerce in Houston. West Dallas Street became the heart of Houston's black business district. By the 1920s over 95 percent of the city's black-owned businesses were located in this neighborhood. [3] The Fourth Ward neighborhood also became the social and cultural center for black Houston (see Map 5.1).

The depression contributed to the gradual erosion of black land ownership in the Freedman's Town/Fourth Ward neighborhood. However, the neighborhood's population base continued to expand during the 1940s. The housing pressures created by this expanding population contributed to the growth of the city's other predominantly black wards (i.e., the Third

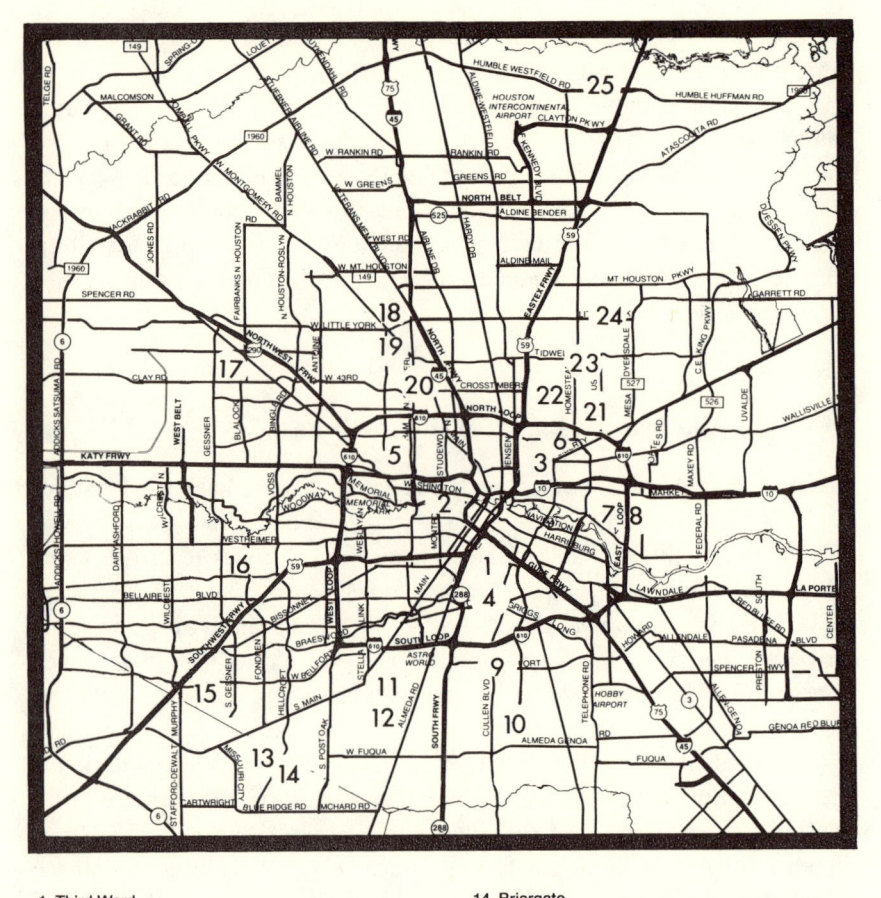

1. Third Ward
2. Fourth Ward
3. Fifth Ward
4. Foster Place/MacGregor
5. West End
6. Kashmere Gardens
7. Pleasantville
8. Clinton Park
9. Sunnyside
10. South Park
11. Almeda Plaza
12. Hiram Clarke
13. Chasewood

14. Briargate
15. Riceville
16. Carvercrest-Pineypoint
17. Carverdale
18. Acres Homes
19. Shepherd Park
20. Studewood Heights
21. Settegast
22. Trinity Gardens
23. Scenic Woods
24. Northwood Manor
25. Bordersville

Map 5.1   Predominately black Houston neighborhoods, 1982. (Base map by Key Maps, Inc., lic. no. 93.) From *Invisible Houston: The Black Experience in Boom and Bust*, by Robert D. Bullard. Published by Texas A & M University Press, 1987.

Ward and the Fifth Ward). By 1950, for example, the Fifth Ward was Houston's largest black neighborhood. Blacks in the 1960s began moving northward from the Fifth Ward and southward from the Third Ward. The concentration of the city's black population along these corridors (i.e., northeast and southeast Houston) can still be found today.

Houston's Fifth Ward has a rich cultural history and replaced the Fourth Ward as the center of black business and economic activity by 1950. The Lyon Avenue Commercial Corridor was a thriving retail district that prospered under the segregated system. However, the social and economic vitality of the area was severely disrupted with the completion of two major freeway systems (I-10 and U.S. 59 highways), which physically divided the community and isolated its residents from its business core. In addition, out-migration of the young and more affluent residents from the area and the closure of area businesses accelerated the economic decline of this once thriving black community.

The decline of the Fourth and Fifth wards allowed for the emergence of the city's Third Ward. Beginning in the 1960s the Third Ward became the hub of Houston's black social, cultural, and economic life. The mostly black Third Ward, however, is a neighborhood of contrasts where row or "shotgun" houses can be found within blocks of well-manicured, tree-lined estates. The larger Third Ward area incorporates the MacGregor neighborhood, an area that residents commonly refer to as the "richest black neighborhood in Texas." The Third Ward in recent years has experienced an in-migration of young and affluent "urban pioneers." The rediscovery of this neighborhood has intensified the competition between incumbent residents and new arrivals for the area's limited housing stock. The external pressures that were exerted on the Third Ward neighborhood peaked during the 1970s, when housing demands were greatest.

Like other people who relocated to the city, black migrants to Houston sought work and residential opportunities. Booster campaigns in the first decades of the twentieth century promoted Houston as a city in which blacks could expect "unexcelled industrial opportunities."[4] The *Houston Informer*, a black weekly newspaper, took an aggressive posture in "selling" blacks on "Heavenly Houston."[5] In spite of the image, the growing population of black workers and their families intensified the prejudices of whites, resulting in the enforcement of Jim Crow laws institutionalizing racial discrimination. White racism permeated every social and economic institution in "Heavenly Houston." There existed "two separate societies —black and white—connected only by economic necessity."[6]

Neighborhoods in Houston as well as in most other American cities

are not scattered randomly over the urban landscape. Black and lower-income neighborhoods often occupy the "wrong side of the tracks" and consequently receive different treatment. The social and spatial groupings that emerge in urban areas are a result of the "distribution of wealth, patterns of racial and economic discrimination, access to jobs, housing, real estate practices, and a host of other variables."[7] As we noted in Chapter 1, Houston and other Sunbelt cities during the 1970s were heralded as growth centers in the region. But minority populations have been ignored in much of this analysis.[8] The emergence of Houston as a major city can be attributed largely to a number of demographic and economic factors, including weak labor unions, cheap labor, cheap land, and aggressive booster campaigns.[9] While Houston became a mecca for thousands of whites and nonwhites seeking new job and housing opportunities in the 1970s, much of the material written on this era provides only a superficial coverage of the city's racial and ethnic diversity. This was especially true for institutional promoters of Houston. Such promotions treated the city's minority community as an "invisible" community. This is not a small point when one considers the fact that blacks and Hispanics composed over 45 percent of the city's population in 1980.[10]

Early booster campaigns promoted Houston as the "Magnolia City," the "Bayou City," and "Heavenly Houston."[11] However, the 1980s have seen the economic bubble burst for many Houstonians. This period has also seen a worsening in the condition of the city's poor and unemployed households, for whom Houston has long been less than a perfect home.[12]

The black media have participated in the diffusion of booster-oriented information in their rating of the best cities for black workers and their families. However, the rating schemes of many black publications have gone beyond the mere promotional campaigns in their inclusion of social, economic, and selected demographic factors as key ingredients in their evaluation. For example, the size and shape of a city's black community and the local stratification system are viewed as important variables affecting black mobility. Thus, it seems that images generated by the self-promotion campaigns of local communities and those generated by black institutions are not always parallel.

To fully understand how these conflicting images emerged, one needs to assess the impact of institutional racism on the social structures in which these images are created. A case in point is the systematic omission of black institutions from promotional material. For example, it is not uncommon to find promotional maps of Houston that show the location of the University of Houston but not Texas Southern University. These two state

universities are physically adjacent to each other, separated only by Scott Street, which historically has served as an unofficial line of demarcation between the predominantly white and predominantly black state-supported institutions.[13]

The City Within the City

Houston's black community is indeed a distinctive city within the larger Houston community. This fact is highlighted by the social and demographic changes that have taken place in the nation's fourth-largest city.

Population and Housing Patterns

The Houston metropolitan area comprised almost 3 million persons in 1980, of whom over half a million were black. The city of Houston included some 1.6 million persons, over 440,000 of whom were black.[14] Houston's black community was the fastest-growing black community in the South; the city's black population increased by over 39 percent between 1970 and 1980 and is the largest black community in the South.

The Houston metropolitan area led the nation in housing starts in the 1970s, with over 487,000 new housing units built between 1970 and 1980. Many lower-income and minority neighborhoods were passed over during the peak period of Houston's housing boom, when much of the new housing construction was in the suburbs.

Houston's black community is located in a broad belt that extends from the south-central and southeast portions of the city into the north-central and northeast sections of the city. The black population is largely located in the eastern half of the city, with smaller enclaves in northwest and southwest Houston. While growing in size, Houston's black population has also become more dispersed.

The boundaries of the city's black community have been extended beyond the traditional black areas away from the Central Business District, but blacks remain residentially segregated. The 1980 index of dissimilarity revealed that over 81 percent of the city's blacks would have to move into white areas for the city to eliminate racial segregation; the percentage was higher, at 93 percent, in 1970.[15] Overall, Houston's black population remains residentially segregated in older inner-city neighborhoods that have been historically black as well as black neighborhoods that have recently undergone racial transition due to white flight.

Black Suburbanization   The demand for single-family homes has resulted in the growth of areas outside central Houston. Moreover, new housing constructed in suburbs opened up ownership opportunities primarily for whites, middle-income households, and former homeowners who had accumulated equity capital for down payments. Many lower-income and minority households were passed over during the housing boom of the 1970s. Recent housing trends suggest that as the market tightens, housing options become more limited. This is true for central-city as well as for suburban residents. However, mobility patterns for lower- and moderate-income blacks point to resegregation of this group in suburban enclaves.

While Houston's blacks have gradually moved into the suburbs, in the past two decades their representation among suburban residents has actually declined. For example, the black share of Houston's suburban population dropped from 12.9 percent in 1960 to 8.8 percent in 1970; blacks constituted only 6.2 percent of Houston's suburban population in 1980 (see Table 5.1). The 80,000 blacks in Houston's suburbs represent a far smaller number than might be expected from the size of the central-city black population of more than 400,000.[16]

Black suburbanization has often meant successive "spillover" from predominantly black areas or an extension of the segregated housing pattern that has typified the central city. Many suburban neighborhoods that were racially integrated in the 1970s have become mostly black in the 1980s. This pattern of racial transition is typified in many southeast and northeast Houston neighborhoods that were in the direct path of black residential expansion. Black Houston residents often become resegregated or "ghettoized" in suburbia. In other cases the city's older black suburban enclaves, which were semirural in character (i.e., Riceville, Bordersville, Carvercrest, Carverdale, Acres Homes), have been encircled by new residential and commercial construction with few amenities—paved streets, sewer and water hookups, regular garbage service, and other routine municipal services.

A case in point is Riceville, an all-black suburban enclave, which was annexed by the Houston City Council in 1965. The neighborhood dates back to the 1850s as a rural farm community. However, as late as 1982 this small black community in the rapidly growing southwest sector of Houston did not have running water, sewer or gas connections, sidewalks, paved streets, or regular garbage service.

The Bordersville community is another black suburban enclave neglected by development interests. Bordersville is an all-black neighborhood that grew out of an old sawmill settlement, or "sawmill quarters."

Table 5.1 Black population change in five
southern cities and their suburbs, 1970–1980

Central cities	Black population, 1980	Percent change in black population, 1970–1980	Percentage of blacks in central city	
			1970	1980
Houston	440,257	39.1	25.7	27.6
New Orleans	308,136	15.3	45.0	55.3
Memphis	307,702	26.9	38.9	47.6
Atlanta	282,912	12.1	51.3	66.6
Dallas	266,000	26.3	24.9	29.4

Suburbs	Black population, 1980	Percent change in black population, 1970–1980	Percentage of blacks in suburbs	
			1970	1980
Houston	80,000	21.4	8.8	6.2
New Orleans	79,000	40.4	12.5	12.6
Memphis	37,000	−18.4	31.7	21.0
Atlanta	179,000	222.4	6.2	14.2
Dallas	50,000	35.4	5.2	4.7

Source: U.S. Bureau of the Census, *Census of Population and Housing* (1981).

Houston annexed this northeast community in the mid-sixties as part of its bustling Intercontinental Airport. The problems in this all-black neighborhood are not unlike those found in Riceville, which lies nearly 30 miles to the south—lack of running water, sewer lines, paved streets, regular street repairs, and other neighborhood amenities that other Houstonians take for granted. Bordersville residents in the early eighties had to get their water from a "yellow city tank truck that made deliveries three times a week, charging $2.98 per month for all the water deliveries." [17] The future of this neighborhood is clouded by the fact that few of the residents have clear title to property on which they live (i.e., many of the current residents are descendants of the laborers who worked at Edgar Border's sawmill and lived in the "sawmill quarters"). Moreover, increased pressure has come to bear on Bordersville, as it straddles one of the most affluent areas of Houston, the FM 1960 area, and the rapidly growing north Harris County areas near the Intercontinental Airport.

Home Ownership Black home ownership continues to lag behind the national home ownership rate.[18] Over 64 percent of the nation's families owned a home in 1980, while 44 percent of the nation's blacks were

homeowners. Blacks in the South are more likely to be homeowners than are blacks in any other region. Over one-half of the blacks in the South own their homes; this compares with 44 percent in the North Central region, 40 percent in the West, and 31 percent in the Northeast.[19] Recent housing data reveal that nearly one-half (47.2 percent) of Houston-area blacks own their homes, as compared with about two-thirds (62.8 percent) of the whites in the area.[20]

Low property-ownership rates in many lower-income and black neighborhoods by incumbent residents can be seen as a major obstacle to stabilizing these areas. The by-product of many neighborhood revitalization strategies has often been the displacement of incumbent residents.[21] Houston's historically black wards (i.e. the Third, Fourth, and Fifth wards) are prime examples of inner-city neighborhoods under siege.[22]

Housing Market Discrimination   It has been 20 years since the Federal Fair Housing Act of 1968 prohibited racial discrimination in housing, but blacks still receive unequal treatment in the housing market. Institutional discrimination in the housing industry artificially restricts home ownership options to blacks and thereby denies them the benefits of tax savings and long-term investments. The practices of refusing to sell or lease housing to blacks, coding records and applications to indicate racial preferences of landlords, selective advertising, redlining, racial steering, and threats or acts of intimidation continue to limit the housing alternatives available to black families.[23]

The federal commitment to the enforcement of fair housing laws has weakened in recent years. Moreover, financial and personnel "support to rigorously pursue fair housing efforts have been inadequate to meet the nation's need in this critical area of civil rights." [24] There is clear evidence that the nation's fair housing laws have not been enforced with the same vigor as used in obtaining compliance to other laws.[25] The low priority assigned to enforcement of fair housing laws translates into higher costs for residential services consumed by blacks and limited residential mobility.[26]

In an effort to promote "open" housing, the city of Houston passed its Fair Housing Ordinance on July 9, 1975; this ordinance created the Fair Housing Division (a city agency housed in the mayor's office). Houston's Fair Housing Ordinance was patterned after the Federal Fair Housing Act of 1968. The local ordinance prohibits discrimination in the sale, rental, or financing of housing, and discrimination in broker services due to (1) race or color, (2) sex, (3) religion, and (4) national origin.

Houston's Fair Housing Ordinance suffers from the same defect as fed-

eral fair housing legislation—enforcement provisions are weak. The local ordinance fails to provide the Fair Housing Division with the necessary enforcement powers to be effective; the Fair Housing Division can only seek voluntary compliance through "conciliation" activities (i.e., formal and informal conciliation). The effectiveness of the local fair housing agency has suffered because of a weakened commitment at city hall. For example, the city agency was staffed with nine full-time employees (four of whom were compliance officers) in 1977. The Fair Housing Division in September of 1984 had only three staff persons—an acting director, a secretary, and one compliance officer. The agency in March 1985 was eliminated as an autonomous division under the mayor's office and combined with the city's Affirmative Action Division.

Houstonians have filed numerous complaints with the Fair Housing Division. Over 1,767 housing discrimination complaints were filed with Houston's Fair Housing Division between 1975 and 1983; over three-fourths of these complaints originated from black and Hispanic households, and complaints were concentrated in the western half of Houston (i.e., southwest and northwest) in neighborhoods that have few minorities.[27]

Discrimination complaints filed with the Fair Housing Division fall into four general categories: (1) formal conciliation, (2) informal conciliation, (3) referral to the Houston city attorney, and (4) dismissal. Over two-thirds of the housing discrimination complaints filed with the Fair Housing Division between 1975 and 1982 were dismissed. The dismissals were usually a result of complaint applications that did not have the necessary signatures, complaints withdrawn by the applicants, insufficient evidence, or housing units that were located outside Houston city limits (the local ordinance only covers housing inside the city's boundaries). The city agency used voluntary compliance as the chief method of resolving the discrimination complaints that were not dismissed. That is, informal conciliation (getting all concerned parties to sit down in an informal setting to resolve the dispute) accounted for about one-fourth of the complaints disposed of between 1975 and 1982. On the other hand, only six complaints were referred to the city's legal department for litigation.[28]

The Crisis of Public Housing   The U.S. Housing Act of 1937 and subsequent Texas enabling legislation led to the establishment of the Housing Authority of the City of Houston (HACH). The city's housing authority is responsible for construction of housing under the low-rent housing program. A two-pronged approach was used in carrying out the early mission of the local housing authority: (1) to clear slums and "blighted" areas, and

(2) to provide decent, safe, and sanitary housing.[29] The early housing authority boards emphasized the slum-clearance provision. Land acquisition for public housing projects was often mired in controversy. Allegations were publicized in the *Houston Post* in 1940 that the city's housing authority board used "slum clearance to capitalize [on] poverty and drive a bargain"[30] in Houston's blighted neighborhoods.

Today Houston's housing authority is the largest of the 40 public housing authorities in the Houston-Galveston area. The Houston Housing Authority had a total of 9,893 units of subsidized housing in its 1983 inventory. A breakdown of the housing authority's subsidized units indicates that it owned and managed 4,077 units of public housing in 15 developments scattered across the city. The housing authority's Section 8 Housing Assistance Payments Program provided rent subsidies for an additional 5,816 housing units. The local housing authority served over 25,000 persons in 1983.[31]

The need for additional units of low-rent and assisted housing in Houston far exceeds the current supply. At least one-fifth of the city's more than 600,000 households are inadequately housed and could qualify for some type of housing assistance.[32] For the past five years the Houston Housing Authority has had an average of 5,000 persons on its waiting list for public housing.

The city's aging and rapidly deteriorating public housing stock represents an additional problem for the local housing authority in its effort to provide decent, safe, and sanitary housing for low- and moderate-income households. These problems are exacerbated by dwindling financial resources, weakened political commitment, and growing citizen opposition to public housing. It is becoming increasingly difficult to build public housing in Houston. Public housing has become a volatile political issue that has the potential to create protests from both suburban whites and inner-city blacks. White suburbanites fear that their neighborhoods will be targets for low-income public housing developments as a result of the federal government site-selection policies restricting new subsidized units in impacted areas (i.e., neighborhoods with large concentrations of minorities and low-income residents); suburban residents also fear that lower-income housing projects would adversely affect their property values and the overall quality of life in their respective neighborhoods. Black inner-city residents, on the other hand, fear that public housing developments are being programmed for failure through a policy of neglect and site locations away from the people who need assisted housing the most (i.e., lower-income households).

A case in point is the 1982 decision by the Houston Housing Authority to approve the construction of two family developments in predominantly white neighborhoods. The housing authority approved the construction of a $5 million 105-unit low-income housing development in the Westbury area. The census tract in which the proposed project was to be built had an ethnic composition of 89 percent white, 4 percent black, and 7 percent Hispanic. The selection of the mostly white neighborhood in southwest Houston triggered protests, demonstrations, and legal action. The proposed project was ultimately killed after the developer had problems securing the $5 million loan to begin construction. Citizen opposition to the proposed development influenced the housing authority to later revise its application to the U.S. Department of Housing and Urban Development from a family development to one that would house elderly persons. An elderly development on the proposed site in the Westbury area would likely generate less controversy than the original proposal for a family development. Historically, the city's assisted family developments have been composed of minority tenants (i.e., blacks, Hispanics, and Indochinese), while the low-rent elderly housing developments are occupied primarily by whites.[33]

Another case involved a proposed public housing development slated to be built in northwest Houston. A $3.5 million 80-unit public housing development was approved in 1982 by the Houston Housing Authority for the predominantly white Spring Branch area. The census tract in which the low-income housing development was to be built is 87 percent white, 4 percent black, and 9 percent Hispanic. Residents of the Spring Branch area were also able to garner enough support at various levels to convince the developer not to purchase land for the proposed project. The housing authority subsequently cancelled the controversial low-income family development planned for this middle-income neighborhood in northwest Houston.

The future of Houston's historic Fourth Ward is often linked to the fate of one of the city's oldest public housing projects—Allen Parkway Village.[34] This linkage is highlighted by the commonly held belief that "as goes Allen Parkway Village, so goes the Fourth Ward." Allen Parkway Village has been the subject of much speculation as a result of its close proximity to the downtown area. The public housing project has experienced a dramatic change in its tenant population beginning in the mid-seventies. Blacks constituted 66 percent of the project's tenant population in 1976, while Indochinese made up only 5 percent. The black tenant population in Allen Parkway Village dropped to 34 percent in 1984, while

the Indochinese (mostly Vietnamese refugees) tenant population increased to over 58 percent of the project in that year. The housing authority's "replacement" policy (i.e., selecting Indochinese over blacks), which began in 1976, appears to have anticipated the demise of Allen Parkway Village as a viable public housing project (see Chapter 4). In addition, the political implications of the housing authority's replacement policy are clear: the demolition of a public housing project that housed primarily Indochinese refugees would cause less political fallout than one that housed mostly blacks. The ethnic composition of the project remained stable in 1983 and 1984. However, only 528 apartments of the 1,000-unit development were occupied in August of 1984. The physical condition of Allen Parkway Village has been allowed to deteriorate over the years to the point that most of the apartments in the development (including many of the occupied units) are not decent, safe, or sanitary.

Policing the Black Ghetto

The Houston police force has a long history of abuse against the city's black workers and youth. A confrontation between police and black citizens frequently raises the question, "How many heads were cracked?" For example, the infamous Houston race riot of 1917 followed "a period of rising racial tension"[35] heightened by an altercation between two white Houston police officers and black military police or provost guards from Camp Logan, a black military encampment that was located near the present Memorial Park site. This violent confrontation between blacks and whites was triggered by the arrest of a black woman by two white police officers; the officers treated the black woman with "considerable severity, if not actual brutality."[36] A black provost guard from Camp Logan attempted to intervene and was subsequently beaten, arrested, and jailed. Another black provost guard from Camp Logan attempted to locate the two Houston police officers to find out what had happened to his comrade and why. After finding the two policemen, the second provost guard was "chased, shot at, captured, and locked up."[37]

In an effort to punish the Houston police for its mistreatment of black military police, a group of 75 to 100 black soldiers from the Twenty-Fourth Infantry seized weapons from the Camp Logan armory and went on a raid in Houston. The August 23, 1917, riot resulted in a death toll of 25 policemen, two white soldiers, four black soldiers, one Hispanic, and eight white civilians.[38] A military court-martial was conducted that was "only a slight pretense of a trial."[39] Thirteen black soldiers were hanged

for murder and 41 received life sentences. Two subsequent trials were held, with an additional 12 soldiers receiving life sentences and 16 receiving the death penalty. Blacks across the country were outraged at the sentences and "many men of the Twenty-Fourth Infantry swore vengeance on the officials whom they accused of unfair treatment." [40] President Woodrow Wilson later commuted 10 of the 16 death sentences to life in prison.[41]

Although many of the social problems that triggered nationwide protest, demonstrations, and riots in the 1960s were present in Houston at that time, the city's black community remained relatively calm during this turbulent period, with only a series of sit-ins and demonstrations from black students at Texas Southern University. In the spring of 1960 students from Texas Southern University staged a lunch counter sit-in at the nearby Weingarten store located on Almeda in the Third Ward. Weingarten closed the lunch counter to keep from serving the black students. The sit-ins spread to Walgreens (located on Main and Elgin) and to the downtown area where Woolworths, Grants, and the city hall cafeteria were targets.

Student demonstrations continued through the mid-sixties, with major on-campus disturbances occurring in 1965 and 1967. The most serious of the disturbances occurred in the spring of 1967, when Houston police clashed with students from Texas Southern University. The violence at the predominantly black university stemmed from police action, protest activities, previous disorders in the city, and the administration of justice. The National Advisory Commission on Civil Disorders classified the disturbance at Texas Southern University as a "serious disorder." [42] The on-campus disorder left one Houston patrolman dead, from a ricocheting bullet; over 480 students were arrested for their part in the disturbance. While the police were clearing the students from the men's dormitory, the officers destroyed several thousand dollars' worth of students' personal property. This overt retaliation by the police intensified the animosity between city hall and the black community.[43]

Further polarization of the black community and police occurred in the early 1970s after the beating deaths of two blacks suspected of auto theft by two white police officers and the killing of 21-year-old Carl Hamilton. Hamilton was the president of a militant black group that called itself People's Party II. A confrontation developed between the police and the group, and Hamilton was fatally shot by the police. The incident, which took place in the Third Ward, is commonly referred to as the "Dowling Street Shootout." This suspicious killing triggered protest from a large segment of Houston's black community. Police Chief Herman Short's resignation was demanded by black protestors, but Mayor Louis Welch did not

remove him.[44] Short's tenure as police chief was marked by controversy, exacerbating the already deteriorating relations between the city's black community and the police.

Relations between police and the black community were enhanced with the 1982 appointment of Lee Brown as Houston's first black police chief despite strong opposition from within the police department. The appointment of Chief Brown by Mayor Kathy Whitmire was perceived as a political victory for the black community. His appointment came just two weeks after the Department of Justice reported that among the 20 largest U.S. cities, Houston was second in number of investigations into civil rights violations by the police. The new chief's administration was marked by increased minority recruitment and special efforts to improve the public image of the Houston Police Department. These strategies have achieved mixed results. The city's police force remains largely white, with blacks making up only 11 percent of Houston police personnel in 1985. In addition, police conduct in inner-city neighborhoods remains a key concern to black residents.

Sharing the Economic Pie
Income, Education, and Employment

Much attention has been devoted to the persisting, even growing, income gap between black and white workers and families in the United States. Black and white earnings had been converging during the early seventies.[45] However, in recent years this trend has reversed. The black-white income gap nationally had narrowed to 61 percent in 1970 and 64 percent in 1974. By 1982 the median family income of blacks had dropped to only 55 percent of that of whites.[46] The median family income for all families in the United States was $19,908 in 1980. Black families in Houston earned nearly 79 percent of the national median (or $15,260).[47] However, white families in Houston had a median family income of $25,699, a difference of $10,439 over the median family income of blacks. Thus, the average black family in Houston earned only 61 percent of its white counterpart. Despite this income discrepancy, Houston's black community is the most affluent in the southern United States. (The median family income of blacks is $13,903 in Atlanta, $13,675 in Dallas, $13,802 in Miami, and $11,798 in New Orleans.)

While black educational attainment has increased over the past four decades, there still exists an educational gap between blacks and whites.

Nationally, the percentage of college-educated blacks increased from 1.3 percent in 1940 to 8 percent in 1980 and 13 percent in 1982. The proportion of whites who had completed college was 5 percent in 1940, 18 percent in 1980, and 25 percent in 1982.[48] Recent census figures on educational attainment in the Houston area reflect the national trend. For example, nearly 42 percent of the blacks in Houston had not completed high school in 1980, compared with 25 percent of the area's whites. On the other hand, a 1985 Rice University study found that white Houstonians are more than twice as likely as their black counterparts to have completed four years of college.[49]

The Houston metropolitan area for the period 1970–1980 was one of the leading centers in expanding job opportunities. Over 669,700 new nonagricultural jobs were created in the area during this ten-year period. The greatest increases occurred in finance, insurance, real estate, services, and the trade industry.[50]

As we noted in Chapter 1, the national recession of the early 1980s had a dramatic impact on the highly touted "recession-proof" Houston economy. The area's white unemployment rate was 6.5 percent in 1982, compared with 11.2 percent for blacks.[51] Houston's black unemployment rate reached a staggering 22.7 percent in 1983, compared with 7.6 percent for whites. The unemployment gap between blacks and whites had widened considerably during the 1982 recession. The black work force in the Houston metropolitan area numbered about 311,680 in January 1983. Black workers made up about 17.2 percent of the area's labor force but constituted over 28.7 percent of the unemployed in metropolitan Houston. Nearly one-fifth (19.2 percent) of the black work force—compared with 8.9 percent of the white work force—was unemployed in 1986.

Black workers in Houston have had difficulty not only in obtaining employment but also in staying employed. Black workers are more likely to be laid off during hard economic times, as they are often the last hired and usually lack seniority or tenure. The problems of the black worker are exacerbated by institutionalized discrimination, cutbacks in social and human resources programs, and a sluggish Houston economy that continues to be heavily tied to oil-related industries.[52]

The distribution of black workers in the local labor market may contribute to their disproportionate unemployment. Black workers were less likely than white workers to be employed in white-collar occupations. Over 63 percent of the whites in the Houston area labor force were engaged in white-collar employment; the figure for blacks was 41.7 percent. Houston's blacks were more likely than whites to be found in blue-collar occu-

pations; 37 percent of the area's blacks were employed in blue-collar jobs, while only 28 percent of the area's whites were blue-collar workers.[53] Blue-collar or manufacturing jobs have not fared well in recent years. The heavy dependence on the shrinking pool of manufacturing jobs is just one example of the economic dilemma facing Houston's black community.

The Growing Underclass

Poverty persists as a national problem. The national poverty rate in 1980 was 12 percent, while over one-third of black families were classified as poor. The poverty rate in Houston was close to the national average. However, over one-fifth of the area's black families fell below the poverty level in 1980.[54] While the black poverty rate is alarmingly high in Houston, it is still lower than the black poverty rates in a number of other major southern and southwestern cities: New Orleans (37.7 percent), Tampa (35.1 percent), San Antonio (29.1 percent), Atlanta (26.0 percent), and Dallas (25.1 percent). The technological nature of the Houston economy may prevent many low-skilled or marginally skilled persons from entering the labor market and thereby escaping poverty. The combination of poor training, low skills, and the changing job market may set the stage for the creation of a permanent underclass that is largely black.[55]

Business and Economic Development

When one talks about economic development, small-business development has to be mentioned. Approximately one-half of the private-sector gross national product (GNP) originates from independently owned businesses with 500 or fewer employees. These businesses make up more than 97 percent of all businesses in the United States and are especially important in the generation of new jobs.[56] For example, between 1969 and 1976 over 96 percent of the new jobs developed in the United States were created by firms with fewer than 500 employees; and more than one-half (52 percent) of these new jobs were generated by business firms with 20 or fewer employees.[57]

Minority business firms have been growing in the past several decades. However, minority businesses are underrepresented in the economic arena. Business ownership rates also differ among the various minority groups. Specifically, the Minority Business Development Agency examined the number of minority business enterprises (MBEs) per 1,000 and found a distribution of 9.2 for blacks, 19.5 for Hispanics, and 28.8 for Asians.[58]

The 1982 data on black-owned businesses in Houston can be found in the U.S. Bureau of the Census *1982 Survey of Minority-Owned Business Enterprises*. For example, Houston had a total of 10,019 black-owned businesses in 1982. These firms had combined gross receipts of $284 million. Houston's black-owned firms are clustered around the services and retail trade areas; these businesses accounted for nearly two-thirds of all black-owned firms in the city.[59]

It is also worth noting that 1983 was the first time that more than one black-owned firm in Houston made the coveted *Black Enterprise* "Top 100 Black Businesses": Smith Pipe Companies, Inc. (ranked 14th) and Frenchy's Po-Boy (ranked 89th).[60] Smith Pipe (an oil supply firm) boomed with the Houston economy. The company in 1980 had sales of over $48 million, making it the seventh-largest black-owned business in the nation. The oil glut and economic recession beginning in 1981 had a dramatic impact on small oil supply firms, including Smith Pipe. The firm's sales dropped to $35 million in 1982; Smith Pipe's 1983 sales totaled less than $4 million, and the company was subsequently dropped from the *Black Enterprise* "Top 100" list. Frenchy's Po-Boy (a fast-food chain specializing in Louisiana Creole-style chicken) has replaced Smith Pipe as the largest black business enterprise in Houston. Frenchy's sales totaled over $8.3 million in 1982 and $9.5 million in 1983.[61] The original Frenchy's is located on Scott Street between Texas Southern University and the University of Houston. This black-owned firm has been expanding since 1979 at the rate of two new restaurants per year. By the summer of 1984, Frenchy's had 11 locations in the Houston area. The economic recessions in 1985 and 1986 forced Frenchy's Po-Boy to close several of the restaurants because of falling sales. However, Frenchy's continues to be one of the largest black-owned businesses in Houston.

The center of black business activity in Houston has shifted over the years with the city's changing residential patterns. The hub of the city's black business and economic life was first located in the Freedman's Town/ Fourth Ward neighborhood.[62] Business activity later shifted to the Fifth Ward, following the city's expanding black population after World War II. Currently, Houston's black financial and business hub is located in the Third Ward. The city's only black bank (Riverside Bank) was located in the Third Ward. Riverside Bank was founded in 1963. The bank, however, became insolvent in 1985 owing to the recession and bad loans. The only black-owned savings and loan association in Texas (Standard Savings Association) is located in the heart of the Third Ward. The Houston Citizen Chamber of Commerce (i.e., the black chamber of commerce), which

was founded in the Fourth Ward, is currently located in the Third Ward. In addition, the Third Ward is the home of Texas Southern University (the third-largest black university in the nation); many of the city's civil rights and black professional organizations are found in this diverse neighborhood.

The pressures that contributed to the economic decline of the city's other black wards are present in Houston's most diverse black neighborhood, the Third Ward. The problems of business disinvestment, redlining, crime, business and residential displacement, and deteriorating housing conditions threaten the continued livelihood of this black neighborhood.

Endangered Environs

Lower-income residents, minorities, and working-class persons are subjected to a disproportionately large amount of pollution in their neighborhoods as well as in their work places.[63] Much of the industry directly responsible for the pollution in lower- and working-class neighborhoods also provides needed employment to the nearby residents.

Moreover, public policies designed to regulate land use and the spatial location of potentially health-threatening externalities (e.g., pollution discharges to the air, ground, and water; noise; landfills, garbage dumps, and toxic waste sites) have a political dimension. Land-use zoning is commonly used as a "protectionist device" to ensure "a place for everything and everything in its place."[64] However, conflicts often result from competing interest groups over the desired outcome of land-use planning.[65] Who gets what and where often depends on the exercise of political power.[66]

Houston is a classic example of how unregulated growth, ineffective land-use controls (Houston is the only major American city that does not have zoning), and discriminatory public policy decisions have allowed an erosion in the quality of residential areas (see Chapter 4). Numerous attempts have been made over the years to institute zoning as a means of land-use control and orderly planning of Houston's growth. However, past attempts have all failed. Houstonians last went to the polls in 1962 in a referendum on zoning; the referendum was defeated. The greatest support for zoning came from upper-income residential areas and the greatest antizoning sentiment was registered by residents of lower-income black neighborhoods.[67]

Houston's neighborhood deed restrictions have served as the primary protectionist device for residential areas. Variable enforcement and re-

newal of deed restrictions in the city's more than 500 neighborhoods have figured largely in the regulation (or segregation) of nonresidential activities. Lower-income and older neighborhoods often have difficulty in enforcing deed restrictions. It is not uncommon for deed restrictions in these areas to lapse, as lower-income residents may be preoccupied with survival and may not have the time, energy, or inclination to get the needed signatures of other residents to keep their deed restrictions in effect. Moreover, the high occupancy turnover and large renter population in many inner-city neighborhoods further weaken the effectiveness of deed restrictions as tools for regulating land use.

While the no-zoning sentiment may be the prevailing view at Houston's City Hall and in development circles, there is mounting evidence that unrestrained growth has its limits. The Houston City Council in the past decade has passed ordinances—a form of "incremental" zoning—that regulate development activities. For example, the city has enacted regulations to deal with development outside the downtown area through its planning commission; it has also enacted controls to regulate new-building setback (the distance between new buildings and major thoroughfares), adult book stores and "sex shops," billboards and advertising signs, sewer-line installations, smoke alarm and wood-shingle roof installations, building in flood-prone areas, junk and salvage yards, garbage dumps and solid-waste sites, and a host of other activities.

A 1983 study of 102 randomly selected Houston civic club presidents, both nonwhite and white, demonstrates a shift toward a prozoning stance.[68] This survey revealed that zoning was endorsed by nearly two-thirds of the respondents; the greatest support for zoning came from minority civic club leaders (over three-fourths endorsed zoning as a land-use device needed in Houston). This study also analyzed environmental concerns by neighborhood location and found that representatives from northeast Houston neighborhoods rated their environmental problems as more severe than did representatives of other sections of the city. Air and water pollution and encroachment by business and industry into their residential areas were considered to be severe problems by over three-fourths of the civic leaders from northeast Houston. In addition, over one-half of the northeast civic club presidents rated noise, litter, trash, and crowding as severe problems in their neighborhoods. Much of the city's heavy industry is located in northeast Houston. Many of the neighborhoods in the northeast sector lie in the direct path of industrial expansion. In other cases the introduction of nonresidential activities (i.e., garbage dumps and landfills) into residential areas has had a destabilizing effect on these areas.

Table 5.2   City of Houston waste-disposal-facility site locations

Neighborhood	Location	Number of city sites		Community development target areas[a]	Ethnicity of neighborhood[b]
		Incinerator	Landfill		
Fourth Ward	Southwest	1	1	Yes	Black
Cottage Grove	Northwest	1	—	Yes	Black
Kashmere Gardens	Northeast	2	—	Yes	Black
Sunnyside	Southeast	1	2	Yes	Black
Navigation	Southeast	1	—	Yes	Hispanic
Larchmont	Southwest	1	—	No	White
Carverdale	Northwest	1	—	Yes	Black
Trinity Gardens	Northeast	—	1	Yes	Black
Acres Homes	Northwest	—	1	Yes	Black

[a] Target areas are designated neighborhoods under Houston's Community Development Block Grant Program.

[b] Ethnicity of neighborhood represents the racial/ethnic group that constitutes a numerical majority in the census tracts that make up the neighborhood.

Source: R. D. Bullard, "Endangered Environs: The Price of Unplanned Growth in Boomtown Houston," *California Sociologist* 7 (Summer 1984): 95.

In their quest for quality neighborhoods, minority and nonminority individuals often find themselves competing for desirable neighborhood amenities (good schools, police and fire protection, quality health care, land-use regulations, etc.) and resisting outputs valued as disamenities (location of sewer treatment plants, waste disposal facilities, public housing projects, etc.). A case in point is the mounting controversy surrounding the disposal of municipal solid waste or city garbage. It seems that all residents want their garbage collected but no one wants it disposed of near their home or neighborhood. Public officials are finding that solid-waste management can become a volatile political issue. Controversy often arises when disposal sites are not equitably located in different quadrants of the city, which would distribute the burden and lessen the opposition.[69]

Houston's landscape is replete with garbage dumps, landfills, and other solid-waste disposal sites. However, the burden of having a waste disposal facility near one's home has not been equally shared by the city's more than 500 neighborhoods. For example, the city over the past 50 years has used two basic methods to dispose of its solid waste: incineration and landfills. Table 5.2 illustrates the location of Houston's city-owned waste disposal facilities from the late twenties through the early seventies. A

total of 13 disposal facilities were operated by the city. The city operated eight garbage incinerators, of which six (75 percent) were located in black neighborhoods; one incinerator was located in a Hispanic neighborhood and one in a white neighborhood.

On the other hand, the city operated five sanitary landfills. All five were located in black Houston neighborhoods. While blacks make up just under 28 percent of the city's population, over three-fourths of the city-owned waste disposal facilities are located in black neighborhoods. Lower-income areas, or "poverty pockets," also have a large share of the city-owned waste disposal facilities. Of the 13 waste disposal sites, 12 (or 93 percent) were situated in designated Community Development Block Grant (CDBG) "target areas." The city's Community Development Program designates neighborhoods to receive federal moneys through the U.S. Department of Housing and Urban Development based upon poverty level, housing conditions, crowding, income, and general physical conditions of these low-income areas. Houston has 25 CDBG target areas. Seven of these target areas have all but one of the city-owned waste disposal facilities. These data clearly indicate that black and low-income neighborhoods have been used as the dumping grounds for the city's solid waste.

The private waste disposal companies appear to have taken their lead from the waste-disposal-facility siting pattern that was established by the city. For example, three-fourths of the privately owned sanitary landfills in Houston (i.e., those permitted by the Texas Department of Health to receive municipal garbage) are located in predominantly black Houston neighborhoods. Thus, waste-disposal-facility siting by both government and the private sector has followed the path of least resistance. This has often meant that public officials and private industry representatives (most of whom are white) have unofficially zoned the black Houston community as suitable for garbage dumps and sanitary landfills.

Conclusion

There can be little doubt that the economic, housing, and population gains experienced by Houston over many decades were the envy of many cities. While such attention has been focused on the growth aspects of the Houston "success story," the differential, often negative impacts of unregulated growth on nonwhite workers and minority families within the city have been severely neglected. This has largely been due to the white elite's aggressive self-promotion and image management campaigns. These booster

campaigns have tended to minimize the ethnic diversity of the city, especially Houston's black community, the largest in the South. The black community in a sense remains an "invisible" community, waiting to be discovered.

While black Houston did benefit somewhat (although to a lesser degree than the larger community) from the expanding educational, economic, and housing opportunities in the seventies, the recessions in the early eighties exacted a heavy toll. Moreover, black Houston has had to bear the burden of the city's growing solid-waste problem. The benefits and the burden derived from the city's period of prosperity have not been uniformly distributed across the city's various groups of workers and their families. Unemployment, for example, has been much more serious for black than for white workers, a condition that has not really changed since the nineteenth century. In recent years discriminatory public policy decisions, ineffective land-use regulations, and the absence of long-range urban planning strategies have contributed to the disproportionate share of environmental degradations experienced in Houston's black community.

While much attention has been focused on the growth and boom aspects of the Houston area, many concerns of the black community have gone unnoticed or have intentionally been de-emphasized. The problems that confront black Houstonians are not unlike those that confront other urban blacks in the United States. Specifically, inadequate housing, declining neighborhoods, unemployment and underemployment, disinvestment and redlining in inner-city neighborhoods, underrepresentation of blacks in the business arena, and the absence of a coherent community and economic development master plan for the black community are issues that confront virtually every black community in the nation.

Black Houstonians have been joined since the early 1900s by a growing population of Hispanic workers and their families. Together with the black population, Hispanics provided much of the labor required to build this massive city. It is to the Hispanic communities that we now turn.

6

Patterns of Racial and Ethnic
Disparity and Conflict:
Hispanic Communities

As Houston developed as a major center of railroad and cotton specialization and, later, oil-industrial specialization, its population of Hispanic
workers and their families grew dramatically. Since the early 1900s economic development in Houston has involved an infusion of Hispanic energy
in the form of thousands of workers. As in the case of black Houstonians,
we again see that the urban growth machine does not run solely on the
fuel of capital but mainly on the energy of the city's workers. Moreover,
the case of Hispanic workers demonstrates the global context and global
connections of the "capital of the Sunbelt." [1] From the early 1900s to the
1980s, Houston has drawn heavily on migrating workers from Third World
regions, particularly Mexico and more recently Central America. Since
World War II these Hispanic migrations have grown significantly, providing the city with much-needed labor to build and service its oil-centered
industries. Rhythms of migration flows have paralleled investment flows.

This description and analysis of Hispanics [2] in the Houston area provides
a sociohistorical account of population development and a discussion of
growth statistics from three structural viewpoints; a review of the growth
and distribution of Hispanic communities; a detailed analysis of the employment, income, and educational conditions of Hispanics, whites, and
blacks in the metropolitan area; and an overview of Hispanicization in the
city.

Throughout the chapter we emphasize Houston's Hispanic immigration.
The large-scale influx of Mexican and other Hispanic immigrants, at one
of the highest levels in the country, has been a significant factor in the
dramatic expansion of the Houston area's Hispanic population. This immigration presents an important contrast between the growth dynamics of
the area's Hispanic and black communities.

The Historical Background: Laboring for Houston

As is true for black Houstonians, the development of Houston's Hispanic population as a supply of low-wage labor goes back to the founding of the city in 1836. According to the historian F. Arturo Rosales, Mexican prisoners taken at the Battle of San Jacinto were forced to work with black slaves in the clearing of the swampy lands along Buffalo Bayou in the Allen brothers' preparation for Houston's land development.[3] In the late 1800s some Tejano (Mexican) families who were forcibly displaced from their lands by white settlers located in Houston.[4] It was the city's railroad and shipping development, linked to the city's growing role as an agricultural marketing center, that made the area a significant destination for immigrant Mexican workers. By 1910 several hundred Mexican immigrants labored in the city's railroad yards and on ship channel construction.[5] In the 1910s Southern Pacific employers in the city obtained hundreds of immigrant Mexican workers from labor agencies in San Antonio. With the additional immigration of working-class and a few middle-class families fleeing the Mexican Revolution, Houston's Hispanic population emerged as a viable community in the 1920s. With over half of its residents coming from the Mexican states of Nuevo León, Coahuila, and San Luis Potosí, El Segundo Barrio (located in the Second Ward) developed east of the downtown district of Houston, and concentrated around Our Lady of Guadalupe Church, as the initial Mexican community in the city.[6]

Further immigration in the 1920s led to the development of Magnolia as the city's largest barrio. In El Segundo Barrio, Mexican workers were primarily employed by Southern Pacific for $2.50 a day. In the barrio of Magnolia, Mexican men were heavily employed in cotton compresses, cement plants, and construction companies, and the women in textile plants.[7] The barrio of Magnolia attracted Mexican-Americans from many localities in Texas. Many Mexican-Americans in the state regarded this barrio as a city in itself, affording numerous job opportunities.

By the 1930s Mexicans in both barrios lived in a sociocultural environment that included ethnic churches, social societies, ethnic business enterprises, Spanish-language newspapers, Mexican national festivals, and a strong sense of Mexican cultural tradition. Like the black community, the Mexican-origin barrios became a city within the city.

The depression, however, slowed the growth momentum of the Mexican community. By the time of this economic downturn, the Houston Mexican-American community had three main social classes: a small group of professionals and merchants, the long-time working-class residents, and the

newly arrived unskilled laborers.[8] The depression caused special pressure for the latter two groups as well as for blacks, as some job programs advertised for white Americans only. Although Mexican immigrants rounded up by the local police were deported by the federal government, Houston's Mexican community did not experience the massive deportation of Mexicans that occurred in Los Angeles and in other areas of the country during the depression.[9] An important reason for the absence of repatriation hysteria in Houston was the vitality of the oil industry, which spared the city the most severe economic hardships experienced in other urban areas.

Though not subjected to massive repatriation, Hispanics in Houston did experience other forms of social conflict. As throughout Texas, much of Jim Crowism was extended to Houston's Hispanic population. Discrimination against Hispanics pervaded all major institutions in the area. Similar to the experiences of the black community, relations between the Mexican-American community and the city's police department were often tense. Several leaders in the Mexican-American community made efforts to combat the prejudice and discrimination faced by Mexican-Americans in the city.

One of the efforts involved the founding of the League of United Latin American Citizens (LULAC) Council #60 in Magnolia in 1934. In the 1930s the Magnolia Council focused on the problems of low Hispanic employment with the city, police brutality, and juvenile delinquency. A women's auxiliary group was formed in 1935. Both the Magnolia Council and the women's group recruited working-class and middle-class members, especially from Mexican-American social and sports organizations. In 1939 Council #60 moved its meetings to a more central location in a downtown courthouse.

During the 1940s LULAC leaders actively and openly opposed segregated schools and police brutality in the Houston area. The struggle for equality and civil rights remained a constant feature of the LULAC councils in the Houston area, which numbered more than 10 by the 1960s.[10]

Based on historical sources and on the 1970 and 1980 censuses, the growth of the Hispanic population in the city of Houston since 1900 can be approximated as follows:[11]

Year	Population
1900	1,000
1908	2,000
1920	6,000
1930	15,000

1940	20,000
1950	40,000
1960	75,000
1970	150,000
1980	280,000

The figures from 1900 to 1940 approximate the Mexican-origin population, which accounts for nearly all Hispanics in the city. Figures for 1950 to 1980 represent Spanish-language, Spanish-surname, or Spanish-origin residents. Even at the time of the 1980 census, the Mexican-origin population represented an overwhelming majority (88 percent) of the city's Hispanics. It is important to keep in mind that the figures do not include the total undocumented Hispanic population in Houston.

Hispanic growth in Houston in the post-1940 era paralleled the area's increasing importance as a center of oil-technological specialization in the world economy.[12] The explosive post-1950 Hispanic growth occurred at a time when Houston was first in the country in capital expenditure in manufacturing (1950s), first in port tonnage in foreign trade (1970s), and first in the number of foreign bank firms outside of New York.[13] By the 1970s Houston's Hispanic working class had greatly diversified its occupational statuses, in comparison to the early days of Mexican workers in El Segundo and Magnolia barrios.

Hispanic Political Powerlessness

Paralleling the experience of blacks in the city, Hispanics have remained politically powerless for most of their existence in Houston. Even with dramatic Hispanic growth, there was no Hispanic representative on the city council until 1979, when the city council election system was changed from eight members elected at-large to nine members elected from districts and five at-large. This change came about because the U.S. Department of Justice ruled that the city's annexations of outlying white areas in 1977 and 1978 diluted the city's minority voting strength, a violation of the Voting Rights Act. For the annexations to be legally acceptable, the city was required to have some council members elected from districts, ensuring minority representatives from black and Mexican-American districts.

Blacks, Hispanics, and other minority political groups in the city formed the Citizens' Coalition for Responsive Government, which sought a council makeup of 16 members elected from districts and 4 elected at-large.[14]

For the Citizens' Coalition, enlarging the size of the city council increased the opportunity for minority interests to be represented in city government. The incumbent mayor and eight council members and the business sector favored the 9-5 plan. Houston Chamber of Commerce leaders argued that a 16-4 plan would lead to fragmentation in the city government. The 9-5 referendum was passed by a 64.4 percent majority in August 1979.[15] In the first city election under the new plan in November 1979, Ben Reyes, a former state representative and the son of a Mexican immigrant worker, was elected the city's first Hispanic council member.

Hispanic political influence in the Houston independent school district has been just as meager. It was not until 1972 that a Hispanic, David T. Lopez, served on the nine-member Houston school board. Like Ben Reyes, Lopez was the son of Mexican immigrants. He was followed on the school board by Tina Reyes, Ben Reyes's sister, who has served on the board since 1981. By comparison, there are three black school board members. For Hispanic students, as well as for black students, lack of an adequate minority representation on the school board was costly. To illustrate, from 1948 until 1967 the trustees refused to use federal moneys of the National School Lunch Act to provide free lunches to indigent schoolchildren. For close to 20 years many needy schoolchildren went without a noon meal because a majority of the school board members viewed free lunches as a road to the welfare state and, thus, a barrier to self-reliance.[16] Indeed, the trustees were so opposed to federal influence in schools that they refused to allow school cafeterias to buy meat requiring federal inspection.[17]

Population Growth in Labor Contexts:
The Global City

Houston's Hispanic population has grown even more dramatically than the city's black population, the largest and fastest-growing black population in the South. The Hispanic population in the Houston area grew from less than 2,000 in 1900 to more than half a million in 1985. This expansion was especially dramatic in the 1960s and 1970s, when the Hispanic population more than doubled in each decade. The growth in the 1970s and 1980s has involved a massive influx of undocumented immigrant workers from Mexico and countries in Central America. With the presence of perhaps 200,000 undocumented Hispanic workers, the total Hispanic population in the Houston area may number over 600,000 in 1988.

Table 6.1   1970 and 1980 Houston metropolitan and city populations

	Metropolitan Houston			City of Houston		
	1970	1980	Percent increase	1970	1980	Percent increase
Total	1,985,031	2,905,353	46	1,232,802	1,595,138	29
Hispanic	212,444	424,903	100	149,727	281,331	88
White	1,375,040	1,888,003	37	755,162	936,676	10
Black	382,382	528,510	38	316,551	441,303	39
Other	15,165	63,937	322	11,362	39,400	247

*Source:*Based on U.S. Bureau of the Census, *Census of Population and Housing: 1970*, Census Tracts, Final Report PHC (1)-89 Houston, Texas, SMSA; and U.S. Bureau of the Census, *Census of Population and Housing: 1980*, Census Tracts, PHC80-2-184 Houston, Texas, SMSA.[19]

As shown in Table 6.1, the growth rate of Houston's Hispanic population in 1970–1980 was well over twice the growth rate of either the white or the black population both in the metropolitan area and in the city. The Bureau of the Census gives a higher population count of blacks than of Hispanics for 1980; however, the Hispanic count does not include the total undocumented Hispanic population.

Taking into account the substantial immigration of undocumented Hispanics from Central America (mainly from El Salvador) in the 1980–1985 period, it is likely that the undocumented Hispanic population in the Houston metropolitan area approached 200,000 by 1985. However, even if we accept a conservative estimate of 100,000, the *total* Hispanic population in the metropolitan area is over half a million, perhaps as much as three-quarters of a million in 1988, taking natural growth into consideration. The Texas Department of Health estimated the Hispanic population in Harris County alone to be 520,000 in 1985.[18] Thus, it is likely that in 1988 the total Hispanic population in the Houston metropolitan area equals the size of the black population (Table 6.1).

What accounts for the high rate of Hispanic growth in Houston? The answer must take into account the threefold context of the development of Houston as a global economic center, the role of foreign migrant workers in U.S. urban areas, and refugee-labor migration.

Growth of the Economy and of the Hispanic Labor Force

As described in Chapter 2, when the Houston metropolitan area became an important center of oil-technology specialization, it established links to regions throughout the world as sources of petroleum for refining in

Houston or as markets for Houston's oil and petrochemical technology.[20] Areas providing petroleum or a market outlet for Houston's oil-industrial complex include Latin American regions in the 1950s and 1960s, Middle Eastern regions in the 1960s and 1970s, and deep-water areas in the Gulf of Mexico, the North Sea, and the Yellow Sea in the 1970s and 1980s.

Sassen-Koob has analyzed the role of Hispanic (immigrant) labor in the restructured economies of urban areas that became "global cities." [21] According to Sassen-Koob, Hispanics are an important source of labor for the growth of low-wage jobs in the service and restructured manufacturing sectors of global cities.[22] In particular, Hispanic workers, along with Asians (and West Indians in New York), provide labor for the nonunion, low-wage jobs with little English-language requirements.

Houston's development as a global center of oil-industrial specialization has strongly affected the metropolitan area's labor market. While the expansion of oil-technological industries directly affected the area's development of oil-related work forces such as those in refineries, pipe companies, and oil-tool factories, it indirectly stimulated the growth of work forces in support and service industries. Important examples of this indirect growth were the enlargements of work forces in finance and management firms and in commercial- and residential-construction companies. In the boom years of the 1970s, 70 percent of the jobs in the Houston area were dependent directly or indirectly on oil and gas industries.[23] During the area's economic slump in the 1980s, this proportion dropped to 60 percent.[24]

The growth of the labor market's primary sector—that is, of skilled, stable, and well-paying white- or blue-collar jobs—is easily measured. The growth of the secondary sector, however, is difficult to assess. This sector of jobs with little skill, low pay, and employment insecurity is a major location of Hispanic, as well as black, workers in the Houston area.[25] Actually, the primary-secondary segmentation of the area's labor market constitutes an interrelated dependency. On the one hand, the expansion of the skilled labor force of office and skilled blue-collar workers creates demands for a low-wage, low-skill work force for service jobs in, for example, restaurants, laundries, and car washes, and also for residential construction. On the other hand, the existence of a low-wage labor force in service and construction industries is conducive to economic growth involving the formation of professional-managerial and skilled blue-collar work forces. That is, a low-wage labor force in industries such as personal services and residential construction helps maintain a lower cost-of-living environment, which in turn helps to keep labor costs down in firms that employ skilled, higher-paid workers.

Table 6.2 1980 Hispanic populations in selected SMSAs

SMSA	Hispanics	Size rank	Percent increase, 1970–1980
Los Angeles– Long Beach, Calif.	2,066,103	1	97
New York, N.Y.-N.J.	1,493,148	2	20
Miami, Fla.	580,994	3	107
Chicago, Ill.	580,609	4	79
San Antonio, Tex.	481,511	5	45
Houston, Tex.	424,903	6	100

Source: U.S. Bureau of the Census, *State and Metropolitan Area Data Book 1982*; and U.S. Bureau of the Census, *State and Metropolitan Area Data Book 1979*.

As indicated in Table 6.2, the Houston metropolitan area ranks sixth in the country in the size of its Hispanic population, according to the 1980 census. However, the census count does not include the total undocumented Hispanic population. If this Hispanic population is taken into consideration, it is likely that the Houston metropolitan area would rank fourth or possibly third. Hispanic Houston's 1970–1980 growth rate of 100 percent is the highest of the metropolitan areas with major Mexican-origin concentrations. If the undocumented Hispanic count is considered, it is likely that Houston's Hispanic growth rate would even surpass Miami's 107 percent figure, which is heavily based on the immigration of Cuban refugees.

Moreover, there is an important difference between Hispanic labor in relation to the global development of Houston and the cases of Los Angeles and New York. According to Sassen-Koob's (1984) analysis, older, established manufacturing industries are declining in Los Angeles and New York, while business-service (e.g., finance, management) and decentralized manufacturing industries are increasing, along with construction and personal services.[26] In this restructuring of the two cities' economies, Hispanic workers have become an important supply of labor for low-wage, nonunion jobs in the service and reorganized manufacturing sectors. As Sassen-Koob describes, Hispanics, particularly immigrants, take such jobs as residential building attendants, workers producing services or goods for specialty shops and gourmet food shops, and cleaners of all sorts.[27] Hispanics in Houston also take these jobs; but Hispanic working-class growth in Houston has not followed a restructuring of the city's economy into a financial and business service center for economic development across the

Table 6.3   Houston metropolitan population
growth rates (in percentages)[a]

Period	Total	Hispanic
1900–1910	38	100
1910–1920	47	200
1920–1930	75	150
1930–1940	42	33
1940–1950	47	100
1950–1960	51	88
1960–1970	40	100
1970–1980	45	100

[a]Growth rates prior to 1950 are based on estimated population figures.

Sources: Joe R. Feagin, "The Global Context of
Metropolitan Growth: Houston in the Oil Industry,"
American Journal of Sociology vol. 90, no. 6 (May
1985); F. Arturo Rosales, "Mexicans in Houston:
The Struggle to Survive," *Houston Review*, vol. 3,
no. 2 (1981); Margarita Melville, *Mexicans in Hous-
ton* (Houston: Center for the Humanities, National
Endowment for the Humanities, 1982); U.S. Bureau
of the Census, *State and Metropolitan Area Data
Book* 1982; U.S. Bureau of the Census, *State and
Metropolitan Area Data Book* 1979.[28]

globe. The growth of Houston's Hispanic population has been dramatic
since the beginning of the city's development as an oil-industrial center
(Table 6.3).

In-migration from rural areas in Texas and from Mexico has been an
important component of the large increases of the Hispanic population
in Houston. This Hispanic in-migration is somewhat similar to the immigration of European working-class people in the industrializing Northeast
during the nineteenth and early twentieth centuries.[29] Hispanic immigration, heavily from Mexico, has been a constant feature during Houston's
industrialization. While Hispanic labor in-migration in other areas of the
United States has followed economic restructuring, in the Southwest it has
been a constant feature of economic development.[30]

The development of the Southwest's agricultural, mining, ranching, and
railroad industries attracted immigrant workers to the region.[31] As the cost
of capital cheapened in the late 1800s, many enterprises in the Southwest
expanded their operations, relying heavily on Mexican migrant labor.[32]
From less than half a million in 1900, the heavily immigrant Mexican

population in the United States grew to about 1.5 million by 1930.[33] Depressed social and economic conditions at home also motivated Mexican workers, as well as more affluent groups, to emigrate to the United States. The turmoil of the Mexican Revolution (1910–1920s), the destruction of communally owned *ejidos,* landlessness experienced by over 96 percent of rural families in many states, famine, and wages of 20¢ to 30¢ per day— all motivated Mexican families to seek a better life in the United States.[34] In the words of Cardoso, "Migration was the only liberation." [35]

From these families fleeing social unrest and economic hardships came many of the early Mexican immigrants to Houston, Mexican families that supplied labor power for the city's early railroad construction ("track labor") and ship-channel-related industries in the southeast side. Letters stored in the Houston Metropolitan Research Center provide glimpses of the experiences, hopes, and aspirations of the Hispanic immigrants in the Houston area. The letters of Victoriano S. Rodríguez to his sister in his Mexican hometown of Aguascalientes from 1929 to 1941 indicate how temporary migrants became permanent settlers, how immigrant families grew, and how the new country was compared with the old one:

(August 18, 1929) I do not doubt that one day . . . I will return to my country where I was born and the land for which I aspire.

(January 28, 1933) All of my sons and daughters are very big now and I, well, I am very old but I still have the desire to return to my country, but this perhaps will not come to be, except if God our Lord wishes that I return even if only to die there. As for this country, it is very sad, there is very little money, due to the lack of needed work many people are almost begging.

(November 10, 1939) Just imagine, from 2 that we were, Jesús and I, 27 have resulted and who knows if there will be more since the children are just beginning.

(June 24, 1941) But I will also tell you that in the United States there are very good hospitals for us, the poor, and they attend the rich as well as the poor.

During World War II workers were brought from Mexico into the Houston area as part of a contract-labor system, the bracero program, developed by the United States and Mexico in 1942.[36] In this labor arrangement, Mexican agencies recruited the contract workers, while U.S. agencies

organized their transportation and employment. Though the bracero program was set up primarily for agricultural work, several thousand contract workers were distributed among railroad companies during World War II to do track labor.[37] The Santa Fe Railroad, which had an office in Galveston, used braceros in the Houston area.

Interoffice communications of the Santa Fe Railroad (e.g., a lengthy memorandum entitled "Hints on the Employment of Mexican Laborers") indicate the serious consideration given to the control of Mexican labor. One important concern was to keep braceros separate from Mexican-American crews:

> We do not want to mix any of our local Mexican laborers in with these men [braceros], as it is our understanding that these Mexican Nationals are, for the most part, from cities and towns and probably of a higher caste than those now in our employ, and it has been decided it will work out to better advantage to keep these guys separate and apart from our local or partly Americanized Mexicans.[38]

The existence of an interoffice memorandum concerning the apprehension of "missing workers"[39] suggests that braceros sometimes abandoned track labor and fled to the cities.

The bracero program also had an indirect impact on the migration of Mexican workers to urban areas such as Houston, Los Angeles, and Chicago. According to scholars of Mexican immigration, many Mexican workers attracted by the bracero program to northern Mexico but not recruited as braceros crossed the border to the United States as undocumented migrant workers.[40] A U.S. government roundup program of undocumented Mexican workers in 1954 apprehended over 1 million.[41]

By the late 1950s there was a massive shift of undocumented Mexican labor from rural industries to urban areas, where these workers found jobs in the least attractive occupations.[42] Though the undocumented Hispanics migrating to U.S. urban areas remain predominantly male, family migration increased in the 1970s and 1980s. In the Houston area the presence of undocumented Hispanic families was highlighted in 1980, when undocumented Mexican parents filed suit in federal court against a Texas law barring the education of undocumented migrant children in public schools.

Foreign Migrant Labor

From the structural perspective of U.S.–Third World relations in the world economic system, undocumented Mexican workers in the Houston area

are part of a new labor system in the advanced capitalist economies. It is a labor system in which low-wage, labor-intensive employers in advanced economies such as those in the United States, France, and West Germany obtain labor from foreign migrant workers, who are substantially restricted from joining working-class movements and can be sent home in times of economic downturns.[43] Moreover, in this migrant-labor system the cost for the production and reproduction of labor power is borne by the country of origin.[44] That is, in this migrant-labor system the use of labor power is separated from the cost of its production (in terms of food, schooling, and health care costs). The increase of undocumented immigrant family households, such as in the Houston area, represents a new phase of this foreign migrant-labor system: the relocation of the reproduction of (foreign) labor power, and its social costs, to the host society.

Social scientists, government officials, and Mexican-American community leaders estimate the number of undocumented Hispanic immigrants in the Houston metropolitan area at 100,000 to 300,000. For example, the director of Centro para Immigrantes, a Houston agency providing low-cost legal services for immigrants, estimates that in addition to about 150,000 undocumented Mexicans in the Houston area, about 140,000 Central American immigrants (refugees) came to the area between 1980 and 1984. He divides the Central American influx to the Houston area as follows: 100,000 Salvadorans, 30,000 Guatemalans, and 10,000 Hondurans, Nicaraguans, and Costa Ricans.[45]

More elaborate estimates have been made of the size of the undocumented Mexican population in the Houston area. Working under the assumption that undocumented Mexican immigration to the United States is male-selective, and using sex ratios derived from the 1980 Mexican Census, Bean *et al.* (1982) estimate undocumented Mexicans in the Houston area at between 80,954 and 130,688.[46] Using a 3 to 1 ratio of Chicanos to Mexican immigrants, Browning and Cullen estimate that there are 100,000 undocumented Mexicans in the Houston area.[47] It is important to understand the differentiation of undocumented Hispanic growth in the Houston area. Based on field studies and on observations by community-service workers, Mexican workers and families constituted a large majority of undocumented Hispanic migration to the area in the 1960s and 1970s.[48] This migration was basically a continuation of historical working-class migration from Mexican regions to the Houston area. The fact that initially many undocumented workers were males and came as temporary migrants demonstrated a new complexity of international migration in which Third World workers periodically migrate to advanced industrial societies, where

they do wage work in order to supplement household income back home.[49] Sometimes this temporary migration is coordinated with the planting or harvesting season at home.[50] Thus, initially the entry of large numbers of undocumented workers to the Houston area in the 1960s meant a change to a *migrant* labor pattern, as compared to the pre–World War II *immigrant* labor pattern, in which the Mexican working-class families became permanent settlers. Yet this contrast should not be stressed too strongly, as field studies indicated a significant presence of undocumented Mexican families in the 1970s.[51]

In the view of some public officials and community-service workers, undocumented Central American immigration in the Houston area in the 1980–1985 period almost reached the level of undocumented Mexican immigration in the 1970s.[52] Regardless of the accuracy of this view, it is clear that the post-1980 undocumented Central American immigration in the Houston area was explosive, making Houston second only to Los Angeles in number of Central American immigrants.[53]

Salvadorans constitute the largest group of Central American migrants to the United States. According to various sources, an estimated 90 percent of the undocumented Salvadoran migrants who make it to the lower Rio Grande Valley intend Houston as their destination in "el norte." [54] The majority of the Salvadorans migrating to the Houston area are from rural origins; many worked as peasant farmers in what are now war-torn zones. Yet some who make the trip of over 1,000 miles come from San Salvador or smaller urban areas, where they were factory workers, truck drivers, and so on.[55]

In Houston Salvadorans settle in several areas. Some are found in the most affluent areas as live-in servants. There are a few areas of concentrated settlement in the traditional Hispanic barrios on the east side and in the city's southwest sector.[56] In some cases Salvadorans from the same town settle in the same apartment complex or in the same neighborhood. Taking low-wage, low-skill jobs, the Salvadorans fare no better than other undocumented workers in the city's labor market. The opening of restaurants specializing in Salvadoran cuisine and the presence of two imported Salvadoran newspapers (*El Diario de Hoy* and *La Prensa Gráfica*) indicate the significance of Salvadorans as a new Hispanic population in Houston.[57]

Refugee-Labor Migration

Salvadoran immigration in the Houston area in the summer of 1980 coincided with the escalation of civil turmoil in El Salvador.[58] Indeed, most

of the first several hundred Salvadoran immigrants detected by community-service workers in Houston early in the summer of 1980 were peasant-farmers from the war-ravaged northern and eastern sectors of El Salvador. Almost without exception, Salvadoran immigrants interviewed in the Houston area by journalists report having been involved in a life-threatening situation in their country. Many tell of relatives, friends, or co-workers who were killed in their country's conflict.[59] For many Salvadorans, therefore, Houston has become an escape from violence at home.

But why have Salvadorans (and Guatemalans) chosen Houston as a sanctuary? Local officials of the Immigration and Naturalization Service (INS) see Salvadoran immigration to the Houston area as motivated by the migrants' desires to find better-paying jobs. According to the view of an INS official in the Houston district, if the Salvadorans were refugees they would stay in refugee camps in Mexico.[60] This view is not without some merit, since there are thousands of Central Americans in refugee camps in Central America and on the Mexico-Guatemala border.

Yet the nature of refugee migration is more complex than a simple relocation process. Refugee migration is a form of labor migration, especially when the refugees are peasants or other working-class people. That is, at the end of their journey refugees must often work to subsist, a fact that is particularly pressing when the refugee unit is the family. It is logical to assume that for refugees areas of greater economic prosperity will be favored as potential destination points. From this perspective, areas in the United States would receive a higher priority as destination points than areas in Mexico, a country with fewer economic opportunities. Los Angeles and Houston are the first two major metropolitan areas of large-scale economic development that Central American refugee migrants encounter after crossing the U.S.-Mexico border. Indeed, Los Angeles and Houston are considered to rank first and second, respectively, in number of Salvadoran immigrants.[61] The large established Mexican communities in these two areas no doubt facilitate the immigration and settlement of Central American refugees, as these communities provide a somewhat familiar cultural environment.

The migration of large numbers of undocumented Hispanic workers to the Houston area has led to anti-immigrant sentiments among many long-term residents. As reflected in letters to the editor in the city's two major English-language newspapers, the undocumented immigrants are viewed as welfare freeloaders, criminals, potential subversives, and usurpers of jobs and educational services. In the worst days of Houston's economic slump, some leaders of local trade unions saw the undocumented as the direct cause of high unemployment in the building industries.[62]

Table 6.4 Houston area distribution
of 1970–1980 population growth (in
percentages)

	City of Houston	Balance of SMSA
Total	39	61
White	15	85
Hispanic	62	38
Black	85	15

Source: Based on the U.S. Bureau of the
Census, the 1970 and 1980 volumes of *Census of Population and Housing*, Census Tracts,
Houston, Texas, SMSA, PHC80-2-184.[63]

Hispanic Communities:
The Geographical Distribution

Like black Houstonians, Hispanics tend to reside in central-city communities. The residential segregation of Hispanics is the result of a number of factors, including historic patterns of anti-Mexican discrimination in the city as well as migrant settlement patterns. While less than half of the white population lived in the central city in 1980, two-thirds of Hispanics were located in this area. The black concentration in the central city is even higher. Since we do not know the distribution of the undocumented Hispanic population between the central city and the balance of the metropolitan area, it is impossible to estimate how this group of 100,000 to 200,000 affects the overall Hispanic geographical distribution in the area. A recent study of undocumented Mexican workers in other Texas metropolitan areas indicated a concentration of these migrants in the central city.[64] Hence, it is likely that the undocumented count in Houston increases the proportion of Hispanics in the central city.

The 1980 distribution of whites, Hispanics, and blacks in the Houston metropolitan area represents over a century of population development, especially for whites and blacks. Table 6.4 gives the groups' differentiated growth for 1970–1980. The figures show a striking contrast between the white and minority growth distribution in the Houston metropolitan area. Most of the recent white population growth occurred outside the central city, while 62 percent of the Hispanic growth and 85 percent of the black growth occurred inside the city. If we consider that the undocumented Mexican population grew rapidly in the 1970–1980 period and that the undocumented Central American population is mainly a 1980–1985 development, then the proportion of the 1975–1985 total Hispanic growth that

occurred in the central city must be substantially higher than 62 percent, since the two undocumented populations are probably concentrated in the central city.

Though Hispanics and blacks have a similar inner-city concentration in the Houston metropolitan area, the two populations differ in concentration levels inside the city. According to 1980 census data, 37 percent of the Hispanics in the city of Houston lived in census tracts where the majority of the population (over 50 percent) was Hispanic.[65] The concentration rate for blacks in the city was 78 percent. Neither one of these figures differs from the 1970 concentration levels by more than 4 percent. These concentration measures indicate that Hispanic residences are more evenly spread in the city, while black residences are generally more concentrated.

Visual observations readily detect the spread of the Hispanic population indicated by census tract data. Hispanics are present in nearly all sectors of the city; major concentrations are found in areas of the city's east and north sides and to some extent in the southwest sector. Observations of areas with a Hispanic presence reveal various degrees of Hispanicization.

An analysis of the extent to which areas are Hispanicized, and hence of the Hispanic expansion process, can be made through a typology of Hispanic zones. The Houston setting is characterized by three types of Hispanic zones: traditional Hispanic zones, zones of Hispanic transition, and new zones of Hispanic settlement. These zones should be interpreted as categories of Hispanicization and not as static classifications.

Traditional Hispanic zones have the highest level of Hispanicization. They are established centers of Hispanic settlement. The traditional Hispanic zones that stand out in the city are the barrios in the east side (e.g., El Segundo Barrio and Magnolia) and in the sector north to northeast of the downtown area. These traditional Hispanic zones are characterized by high levels of Spanish-language usage (especially among adults), Mexican folk culture, Spanish music, and Catholicism. In addition, ethnic self-identities (e.g., "Mexicano" and "Chicano," as opposed to "American") predominate.

In terms of physical characteristics, the traditional Hispanic zones have a large stock of family housing. These are areas that were developed prior to mass apartment housing. Many of the residents in traditional zones are homeowners. The commercial districts in these zones include a large number of ethnic enterprises, such as Mexican restaurants, Spanish record shops, and Spanish-language movie theaters. Even the stores that are not locally owned stock a substantial amount of Hispanic ethnic commodities. Spanish signs pervade the commercial district. Several of the seven Spanish-language newspapers sold in the city can be found in many stores.

What also appears distinctive about the traditional Hispanic zones in the city's east and northeast sides is that they are located near industrial districts. Herein lies a reason for the traditional zones' existence: they emerged as working-class districts. As described above, the original barrios were vital labor sources for the city's railroad and ship-channel-related industries. As such, the traditional Hispanic zones in Houston have a socio-historical commonality with working-class districts in English and other European cities.[66]

Hispanicization in the traditional Hispanic zones is not monolithic. Social and cultural differentiation exists between the zones' Mexican-American, Mexican, and Central American residents. Ethnic differences between the three groups involve such aspects as folkways, dialects, and cuisine. For example, at eating places Mexican-Americans may prefer flour-tortilla tacos, Mexican immigrants the corn-tortilla taco, and Salvadorans the *pupusas*. In the traditional zones, record store owners stock records to satisfy the different musical tastes of the three groups. Only the future will tell what impact the recent Central American immigrants will have on the traditional areas' Hispanicization, which in the past has predominantly been a process of Mexicanization.

The zones of Hispanic transition involve different dimensions and degrees of Hispanicization. These are areas where Hispanics are moving in. Zones of transition contain much of the Hispanic population not concentrated in census tracts. Several zones of Hispanic transition exist a few miles north and northwest of the downtown area. There are other zones of Hispanic transition in the city's southwest sector. The basic dimensions of Hispanicization in these zones involve the movement of Hispanics into the area and the use of the Spanish language in the areas' commercial infrastructure.

Hispanic movement into the transition zones in the city involves Mexican-American, Mexican, and Central American immigrant groups. Needless to say, these groups have adapted differently to the established, English-oriented setting of the area that becomes a zone of transition. For English-speaking or bilingual Mexican-Americans, adaptation is relatively easy; monolingual Hispanic immigrants experience greater difficulty. The complexity of the Hispanic population in an area of transition is also evident in settlement patterns. Mexican-Americans settle in single-family homes, sometimes as home buyers, among white residences; the immigrant Hispanic households cluster in city blocks or in apartment complexes. The sense of Hispanic community found in traditional zones is rarely present.

As merchants and other businesspeople in the transitional areas profit

from the growing Hispanic consumer market, the areas' commercial districts display Spanish advertisements and stock commodities preferred by Hispanic shoppers.[67] Some personal-service firms also undergo a degree of Hispanicization as they hire bilingual staff and advertise in Spanish. "Se Habla Español" signs are displayed in barber shops, insurance firms, and law offices, for instance. Neighborhood 7-Eleven stores start to carry Spanish-language magazines. The commercial districts become further Hispanicized as ethnic enterprises such as restaurants and recreational places open, adding to the districts' Hispanic service work force.

It is difficult to project what the final form and degree of Hispanicization in transitional zones will be. Undoubtedly it will be a condition different from the extensively Mexican traditional zones. Hispanicization in transitional zones involves a combined effect of Mexican-American, Mexican, and Central American immigrant elements. This has a different result from that in the traditional zones, where Hispanic immigrants move into a well-established Mexican-American community. In addition, the level of community control is different. In transitional zones, Hispanics are "outsiders" (and sometimes "undesirables"[68]) moving into areas with educational, religious, and public service institutions that have long been controlled by white residents.

Certainly the level of immigration and economic growth of the city will affect the course of Hispanicization in the transitional zones. If Hispanic immigration declines, Hispanicization may remain at a moderate stage in these zones. But if the city experiences vigorous economic growth, the zones of Hispanic transition may become general transition zones accommodating other groups as well (e.g., Asians). On the other hand, sustained, vigorous economic growth may increase the possibility that transition zones near downtown will undergo de-Hispanicization as developers upgrade the quality of housing for more affluent buyers.[69]

New zones of Hispanic settlement are actually immigrant pockets. Several exist in the city's west side. The new zones have a low Hispanic cultural presence. Their Hispanicization consists mainly of large clusters of immigrant Hispanics in apartment complexes. Indeed, this is the striking characteristic of the new zones of Hispanic settlement—a mass of Hispanic people in a white, English-language environment. Large groups of Hispanic immigrants congregate on sidewalks and parking lots because the apartment complexes they live in have little or no outdoor public leisure space because they were originally designed for people who spend most of their leisure time indoors or in commercial or social establishments.

The Hispanic clusters in the new zones are primarily enclave formations

of undocumented households providing important functions for immigrant settlement. Being denied public social services, the undocumented immigrants develop household mechanisms for economic survival.[70] By developing multiple-family households or forming households in close proximity, undocumented immigrants can reduce housing and other subsistence costs. This especially enables unemployed or undocumented immigrants to survive until a job is found. In addition, the household enclave provides important social functions. Often, many of the families in a household enclave come from the same hometown. This provides the immigrants with a familiar social network of friends or relatives, easing the introduction into the new and strange socioeconomic setting of the city. For many immigrants, social life outside work is contained almost entirely within their enclaves.

Hispanic Communities Outside the Central City

Geographical expansion of the Houston Hispanic population also has been felt in some of the suburbs in the metropolis. But Hispanic suburban growth, like black suburban expansion, deviates significantly from the traditional concept of suburbs as "bedroom" communities from which office workers commute to work in the central city. The major cases of Hispanic suburbanization in the Houston area in 1970–1980 occurred in blue-collar communities—in ones with established Hispanic populations and in others that previously had few Hispanics. Many Hispanics also branched out into traditional white-collar suburbs. But in these suburbs the Hispanic population never reached the levels found in the blue-collar suburbs.

According to the 1980 census, the blue-collar suburbs with over 5,000 Hispanics were Rosenberg, in the western half of the metropolis, and Baytown, Pasadena, and South Houston, in the eastern half, where petroindustrial complexes are located.[71] Also in the eastern half are the blue-collar suburbs with relatively new Hispanic populations: Freeport City, Jacinto City, and Galena Park. In all the blue-collar suburbs the majority of Hispanic workers had manual occupations, with professional and managerial positions accounting for less than 10 percent of the Hispanic work forces. The proportions of Hispanics who worked in the city of Houston ranged from 15 percent in Baytown to 49 percent in Galena Park.[72] Migration out of the central city was definitely not the major source of Hispanic growth in the blue-collar suburbs. With the exception of Galena Park, the number of Hispanics who moved into each suburb from the city of Houston

in 1975–1980 was less than the number who moved in from other parts of the metropolitan area or from outside of it.[73]

Hispanics make up only small segments of the populations of the white-collar suburbs. While Hispanics constitute an average of one-fourth of the population in blue-collar suburbs, they constitute less than half of this amount in white-collar suburbs.[74] In many of the affluent suburbs that developed during the height of Houston's prosperity in the 1970s, few or no Hispanics are present. This is especially the case west of the central city in a business corridor with a chain of affluent suburbs (Hedwig Village, Hunters' Creek Village, etc.). The Hispanics present in the white-collar suburbs contrast sharply with those in blue-collar suburbs. For example, in a white-collar suburb two miles southwest of the city, the nearly 2,000 Hispanic residents have a college-education rate that is five times higher than that in any of the blue-collar suburbs. The level of professional and managerial employment of the Hispanics in the white-collar suburb is three times greater than the highest level in the blue-collar suburbs. In addition, at $28,317, the median family income of the Hispanics in the white-collar suburb is $10,000 greater than the highest median family income of Hispanics in the blue-collar suburbs.[75]

There is a clear relationship between ethnic participation and the geographical distribution of Hispanics in the Houston metropolis. Hispanic ethnic participation is greater in the central city than in the suburbs and greater in the blue-collar suburbs than in the white-collar ones. The existence of the traditional Hispanic zones, whose Hispanic populations are larger than any Hispanic population in the suburbs, and a high concentration of first-generation Hispanic immigrants make the central city the center of Spanish language and Hispanic foods, music, and customs in the metropolitan area.[76]

The blue-collar suburbs, however, may have the highest level of Mexican-American culture. Since proportionately fewer non-Chicano Hispanics are present, Mexican-American culture in these communities is less diluted by other Hispanic cultures.[77] To illustrate, the leading Chicano radio station and dancing places in the metropolitan area are located in suburbs. Indeed, the suburb of Rosenberg seems to be the most active location of Chicano musical culture, as it frequently draws the top Chicano bands in Texas.

White-collar suburbs have the lowest levels of Hispanic ethnic participation. For example, while a large majority of the Hispanic children in the central city and in blue-collar suburbs are bilingual, in the white-collar suburb of Missouri City less than half of the Hispanic children speak Spanish.[78] The absence of Hispanic neighborhoods in white-collar suburbs

limits the social resources for ethnic participation. For example, the Missouri City family of José and María Torres practices ethnic culture mainly on Sundays, when the family attends mass in the old Catholic church in the central-city barrio where José grew up. Usually, the family stays to have dinner with relatives and friends at the house of José's mother. Eric, José and María's seven-year-old son, rarely talks with his grandmother because he speaks only English. His grandmother, a first-generation immigrant, speaks only Spanish.

Some Broad Intergroup Comparisons:
Whites, Blacks, and Hispanics in Houston

Throughout U.S. society, whites fare better socioeconomically than Hispanics and blacks. But Houston's sustained large-scale industrial growth (until the 1980s) and its higher-quality, energy-centered labor market would seem to suggest that if minorities need the "free market" low-wage-labor environment to prosper, then Houston should have been an optimal setting.[79] Yet, as we show below, this has not been the case.

Employment

The employment profile, based on the 1980 census, of whites, Hispanics, and blacks in the Houston metropolitan area is given in Table 6.5. Hispanic workers ranked below whites and blacks in the higher-status white-collar categories. The majority (62.4 percent) of the white-collar Hispanic workers were in sales and clerical jobs. The general pattern for Hispanic workers is a concentration in lower-status manual jobs, as is indicated by Table 6.5. As the percentages demonstrate, Hispanics are more likely than blacks, and over three times more likely than whites, to work as laborers. A 1985 Houston area survey directed at Rice University provides further insight into the relative lower-employment status of Hispanics vis-à-vis whites.[80] The level of full-time employment for white respondents was 62 percent, while for Hispanics it was 57 percent. Blacks ranked third at 51 percent.

According to 1980 census data, there is no major contrast in the upper- and lower-employment statuses among Hispanics in traditional and transition zones in the city. A comparison of the Hispanic work force in a census tract (#311) in a traditional Hispanic zone and one (#511) in a zone of Hispanic transition reveals the percentage of Hispanic workers in white-

Table 6.5   1980 occupational distribution in the Houston area by major group (in percentages)

	White	Black	Hispanic
White-Collar			
Professional/tech-nical/managerial	34	16	12
Sales/clerical	33	26	23
Blue-Collar			
Craft	14	12	22
Operatives	5	8	12
Transport	3	9	5
Laborer	3	8	11
Service	7	21	14
Total	99	100	99

Source: U.S. Bureau of the Census, *Census of Population and Housing: 1980.* Census Tracts, Houston, Texas, SMSA, PHC80-2-184.[81]

collar jobs to be about 25 percent for both tracts. The Hispanic work force of the census tract in the traditional zone had a proportion of 17 percent for the category of handlers, equipment cleaners, helpers, and laborers; the proportion of workers from the census tract in the transitional zone in this category was 14 percent.

The 1980 census information on employment in the Houston area has two important limitations restricting our understanding of the comparative situations of Hispanic workers. One limitation is that there are no refinements of specific categories; hence it is impossible to compare the status of a white manager with that of a Hispanic manager. For example, the white manager could be heading the finance department of a multinational corporation, while the Hispanic manager could be in charge of a neighborhood 7-Eleven store. The second limitation is that the census information does not include the total population of undocumented workers. While some may have been counted, no doubt many were not. If we assume that there are about 150,000 undocumented Hispanic immigrants in the metropolitan area, that half were workers not counted in the census (the rest were unemployed, children, or counted), and that 10,000 of these are clerical workers and the rest evenly divided between blue-collar and service jobs, then the occupational distribution of the total Hispanic work force would be 27 percent white-collar, 47 percent blue-collar, and 27 percent service.

While the true percentages may vary from this projection, it is clear that the proportion of Hispanic workers in the higher-status white-collar jobs is lower than what is indicated by the 1980 census.

The assumption that undocumented Hispanic workers in the Houston area are heavily concentrated in the blue-collar and service industries is supported by the findings of a 1980 exploratory study.[82] The sample of 138 interviews showed that the workers' occupational concentrations were construction (35 percent), service (30 percent), and manufacturing (27 percent). Males had a higher employment rate (94 percent) than females (37 percent). Though the study was not based on a random selection of respondents, its findings are similar to the results of studies in other urban areas in Texas.[83]

Income Status

According to the 1980 census, in terms of income and poverty conditions, Hispanics in the city of Houston were a little better off than blacks but significantly behind whites. The median family incomes of the three groups were whites, $25,699; Hispanics, $16,617; and blacks, $15,260.[84] Within each group the percentages of families with income below the poverty level were whites, 5 percent; Hispanics, 16 percent; and blacks, 20 percent.[85] The 1985 Rice University survey also indicated a similar income disparity between whites and the two minority groups. The reported proportions of household income below $15,000 were whites, 12 percent; Hispanics, 35 percent; and blacks, 33 percent. The surveyed income differences were especially marked in the proportion of household income above $35,000: whites, 51 percent; Hispanics, 23 percent; and blacks, 17 percent.[86]

A comparison of the income conditions of Hispanics in traditional and transitional zones does not yield significant differences. According to the 1980 census, census tract #311, in a traditional zone, and census tract #511, in a transitional zone, had a similar median income of about $14,000. In both census tracts the proportion of families with income below the poverty level was 17 percent.

Again, census data have some limitations for comparing the income conditions of whites, Hispanics, and blacks. The 1980 census predated the social-service cutbacks initiated by the Reagan administration. As a result of the reduced social-service budget, over 408,000 families with dependent children around the country lost welfare-service eligibility.[87] By 1982 over 47 percent of white children and 70 percent of black children in single-parent homes were in poverty.[88] A second limitation of the census

income data is the lack of the undocumented Hispanic count. This is compounded by the fact that the majority of the large undocumented Central American population in the Houston area arrived after 1980.

If the income of undocumented Hispanics is taken into consideration, it is likely that the median income of Hispanic families in Houston is lower than that of blacks. In addition, the Hispanic poverty rate would be higher. As all studies of undocumented Mexican workers have shown, this population exists at the lower levels of income distribution. In the 1980 study of 138 undocumented Mexican immigrants in Houston, the yearly median income was $9,600 in families supporting an average of 5.5 persons.

Education

The employment and income description of Houston Hispanics should give us an idea of the group's educational level, since there is a high correlation among these three variables. In the Houston area, Hispanics have the lowest educational level of the major groups. While 70 percent of the total metropolitan population age 25 or older had graduated from high school in 1980, for Hispanics age 25 or older the proportion was 40 percent.[89] For blacks it was 58 percent. What is especially alarming about the Hispanic figure is that it does not take the undocumented Hispanic population into account. With the presence of this population, the true proportion of the metropolitan area's Hispanics 25 years or older who did not finish high school is substantially higher than 60 percent. The 1985 Rice University survey found a large difference between whites and the two minority groups in the level of higher education. Among white respondents, 34 percent had attended four years or more of college; among Hispanic and black respondents the proportions were 12 percent and 16 percent, respectively.

There are indications that the educational problems of Hispanics in the Houston area will continue not only because the area's fastest-growing Hispanic segment—immigrants—is largely undereducated but also because native Hispanics in general are not faring well in school. The National Commission on Secondary Education for Hispanics reports that across the country some 75 percent of Hispanic students score in the bottom half of standardized achievement tests, and 45 percent of Mexican-American and Puerto Rican students never finish high school.[90] Cultural differences, lack of bilingual teachers, and poor teaching of English are some of the problems usually cited on the schooling side.

In the Houston Independent School District, Hispanics constitute 37 per-

cent of the student population, blacks 42 percent, and whites 15 percent. All of the educational problems described in national reports of Hispanic students are found in the Houston school district. For instance, the school district has a shortage of bilingual teachers. While 90 percent of the school district's teachers are white or black, only 9 percent are Hispanic.[91] The school district has advertised in Mexico and Spain for bilingual teachers. Teachers who can speak Spanish are especially needed in classes with large numbers of immigrant Hispanic children.

To take one concrete example, María Sáenz describes the frustration she and other immigrant Hispanic parents had with a teacher-shortage problem in the fall of 1985: "My two children in the first grade had a different substitute teacher almost every day. I and a group of mothers met with some of the school people to discuss the problem. The mothers were all from Mexico and didn't understand English. The school people said they couldn't find a teacher and so we would have to help teach our children. Then they wrote a list of English words on the board and started to teach the parents how to pronounce them. The mothers just looked at each other. I stood up and said 'It's our job to get the children to school, but it's your job to get them a teacher.' "[92]

While there is also a dropout problem, in the mid-1980s this appears to be true of black and white students as well. In a dropout study, the school district reported that in the 1983–1984 school year 11,050 students dropped out of school; 43 percent were black, 34 percent Hispanic, and 23 percent white. Some curriculum problems faced by minority students 20 or 30 years ago (e.g., being heavily placed in vocational training courses) still exist.

The frustration that Hispanics and blacks have in the area of education was evident in a 1985 survey conducted by the Center for Public Policy at the University of Houston. Forty-eight percent of the Hispanic respondents and 44 percent of the black respondents rated the quality of local public schools as only fair or poor, while among white respondents 28 percent gave a similar response.

Houston's dynamic growth has provided economic opportunity for some of the area's Hispanics. The area's robust job market, especially in the 1970s, enabled some Hispanics to become homeowners and others to become owners of small businesses. But clearly, Hispanics, like blacks, still have a depressed general status in the Houston economy. With the area's downturn in the early 1980s, Hispanic economic conditions became more severe. In the 1985 Rice University survey, 43 percent of Hispanics and 44 percent of blacks picked economic problems over crime and traffic

as the biggest problem in the Houston area. Among whites, 45 percent picked traffic problems. The Hispanic and black educational characteristics indicate a gloomy picture for the groups' future in the area's labor market. In addition, enduring social barriers may also be an obstacle for Hispanic and black mobility in the area's economy. In the Rice survey, a majority of Hispanics and blacks viewed their group's income inequality with whites as due mainly to discrimination.

Conclusion: Some Trends in Hispanic Communities

To understand Hispanic population and socioeconomic development in the Houston area, one must first understand Houston's development as a major oil-industrial center in the world economy. In filling an oil-industrial niche for the global market, the Houston area experienced extensive economic growth. As the area's oil and support industries grew, so did its working class—a working class divided by race and ethnicity.

The distribution of jobs in the Houston area never had a proportional equality among white, Hispanic, and black workers. As throughout the country, the Houston labor market is segmented. This is a historical characteristic of capitalist economies. Just as Irish immigrants became low-status workers during England's industrialization, and eastern and southern European immigrants became low-status workers in the industrialization of the northeastern United States, so have Hispanics, along with blacks, become the critical low-status workers in Houston's remarkable industrialization.

Houston employers have come to depend more and more on the immigrant workers of the area's Hispanic labor force. Thus, to a considerable extent, the Houston economy draws low-wage labor from a transnational labor market—one that extends deep into Mexico and areas of Central America. In regard to Mexico, it has been this way since the 1910s.

Hispanic Population Expansion

As we have seen, Hispanic expansion in Houston has been multidimensional. While there is residential overlap of the different Hispanic groups in Houston, some geographical differentiation exists among the groups. For example, in a northern zone of Hispanic settlement there are many Mexican immigrants who have no ties with the Mexican-Americans in the old barrios on the east side. In the Houston metropolitan area as a whole,

the major pattern of differentiated Hispanic expansion is the overwhelming Mexican-American character of Hispanic growth in the suburbs.

The decentralization of Hispanics in the city of Houston is occurring mainly through sectoral expansion in the eastern half of the city and through multiple-nucleus expansion in the western half. These two types of geographical expansion provide different resources for Hispanic community development. Clearly, sectoral expansion has a considerable advantage for Hispanic community development, since it is a gradual expansion of an already well-established community. Sectoral expansion, thus, is a process of continuity.

Multiple-nucleus expansion, on the other hand, is a process of independent expansion. It is not spatially connected to, and does not necessarily borrow from, a previously established community. Among Houston Hispanics, the exception is that some multiple-nucleus settlers may come from traditional Hispanic neighborhoods in the east side. Given the condition of detached development, multiple-nucleus expansion may further the incorporation of Hispanics in the Houston core society, as Hispanics in these settlements must satisfy many of their daily needs with the resources of surrounding English-language institutions. It is mainly the fast pace of ethnic commercial development and the aggressive Spanish marketing by white retailers capitalizing on the emerging Hispanic consumer market that keep Hispanics in independent settlement areas from being entirely dependent on English-language commercial enterprises.

Hispanicization

Marketing to attract the expanding Hispanic consumer population is one of the evident Hispanic impacts in the Houston area. Especially for the food industry, the Hispanic market means millions of dollars in sales. One supermarket chain in the area, Fiesta stores, has profited greatly from the low-income Hispanic segment. Stocking products geared heavily for this segment, the supermarket chain has expanded to 12 stores of 75,000 to 100,000 square feet, becoming one of the two fastest-growing supermarket chains in the Houston area. Safeway and other large supermarket chains have also opened new ethnic food sections to capture part of the area's emerging Hispanic consumer market. Indeed, plotting the locations of Fiesta stores and other supermarket ethnic food sections accurately indicates the sectoral and multiple-nucleus patterns of Hispanic expansion.

The efforts of some retailers to carry products for specific ethnic groups

within the Hispanic population point to an interesting fact about Houston's Hispanicization. Unlike the Mexican character of San Antonio, the Hispanic texture of Houston is heterogeneous and has a distinctive Latino element. The basis of this urban difference is, no doubt, Houston's global context. That is, in contrast to San Antonio, Houston as a global center has had a more diversified international Hispanic impact.[93]

Houston's Hispanicization is also demonstrated in the growth of Hispanic-owned businesses. These are prolific in the traditional Hispanic zones and are also found in zones of Hispanic transition. Not all of the Hispanic-owned businesses are small operations. A few hire hundreds of workers and have millions of dollars in sales annually. Of the 500 largest Hispanic companies in the United States and Puerto Rico, 14 are located in Houston.[94] The annual publication since 1980 of the *Páginas Amarillas* (the Spanish *Yellow Pages*) demonstrates the growing significance of Houston's Hispanic entrepreneurial sector.

Other important sources of Hispanicization in Houston are the area's seven Spanish newspapers and seven Spanish radio stations. In addition to being an important means for English-speaking businesspeople to reach Hispanic customers, Spanish newspapers and radio stations help the different Hispanic ethnic groups to learn about each other. This function is especially true of radio stations, which continually play the area's various Hispanic musical styles and which have call-in programs for Hispanics to offer opinions on Hispanic issues.

Community Development

Like black newspapers and radio stations in the city's black community, Spanish newspapers and radio stations are important sources for Hispanic community development in Houston. They provide daily information on how non-Hispanic institutions affect the Hispanic community and about the actions of many Hispanic organizations in the city.

The meaning of community development, however, varies among Hispanic leaders in Houston. For Hispanic businesspeople in the east side, community development is viewed in very concrete terms—the revitalization of the old Mexican-American neighborhoods. This perspective combines the goals of neighborhood physical improvement and Hispanic business growth. Efraim Garcia, the city's recent director of planning and development, coordinates the convergence of public and private development resources for revitalization projects in the city's low-income neighborhoods. A result of this program was the development of a Mexican-style

market, El Mercado del Sol, which has the goal of uplifting business activity in a traditional Mexican area adjacent to downtown. For Garcia, who is promoting a citywide "capital improvement" program, this is just the beginning.

Among Hispanic political leaders, Hispanic community development is usually described in terms of increased political power—namely, more voters. The rapid population growth of Hispanics in Houston has not had a proportionate impact in the area's political sphere. Hispanic representation on the city council still consists of the one Mexican-American member first elected in 1979. A young median age, low voter turnouts, and a large number of Hispanic people without citizenship are some of the factors limiting Hispanic political power in Houston.

Some Mexican-American politicos in Houston feel that the city's Hispanic political potential will be realized by the year 2000, when, it is believed, the majority of the Harris County population will consist of Hispanics and blacks (and Hispanics will substantially outnumber blacks in the county). Also, by then the U.S.-born children of the thousands of undocumented Hispanic families in the Houston area will be of voting age.

The expectation of Hispanic political dominance in the year 2000 is overly optimistic. First, Hispanics are a minority in more than just numbers. They are also a minority socially; they have little control or influence over the major institutions (e.g., banks, hospitals, schools) in the Houston area. Voting alone will not be enough to gain political control in the institutional sector. Second, there is the challenge of building political alliances with blacks. Though Hispanics may become the largest group in the county by the year 2000, they alone will not be a majority. Hispanic political goals will require unified efforts with blacks. Finally, there is the question of social-class differentiation within the area's Hispanic population. The Houston Hispanic community in the year 2000 will almost certainly have more social-class differentiation than currently exists. Upper-status Hispanics, who have a higher voting rate, may identify more, and vote accordingly, with a candidate's social class than with the candidate's ethnicity.

Projections of social-class differentiation or any other structural development among Hispanics in Houston must ultimately take into account the historical basis of this population's development—the growth of the Houston area's economy. Competition with petrochemical production in the Middle East, deep-water oil exploration in the Gulf of Mexico, and local production of oil tools for worldwide sales are some of the factors that directly or indirectly affect economic opportunity for Hispanics in Hous-

ton. The near future is not very promising, as economic forecasters predict that a large share of the area's new jobs for the remainder of the 1980s will be in low-paying service industries.[95] While the growth of this low-paying job sector limits the occupational mobility of native Hispanics in Houston, historically it has been an important factor in attracting Hispanics to the area.

In addition, the question of increasing political power has been raised by a variety of Houston communities, including Hispanic, black, low-income white, and middle-income white areas. The social costs of rapid growth in this ostensibly free enterprise city have affected a variety of neighborhoods, minority and nonminority, rich and poor.

7

The Future of the City
Introduction: The Myth
of Independence

Texans and Houstonians have an independent spirit. The grand idea of Texans and Houstonians is that they are so powerful and free that they can consider themselves as independent, somehow separate from the trials and limitations of residents of cities to the north.

In *Seven Keys to Texas* Fehrenbach suggests that the struggle of nineteenth-century Texans to wrest the land from its prior occupants and from the whims of nature inculcated in them certain stubborn traits: "a hard-driving pragmatic business sense, a desperate belief in growth and 'progress' and population increase, and an impatience with most ideologies that did not serve man's mastery over land."[1] Texas and thus Houston symbolize the quintessential American Dream, the place to go to work and do well—to establish oneself without government interference. It is alleged to be the place where a person can make his or her way in the world with little restriction on freedom. It is a place with no significant business taxes and with antiunion laws.

Yet the tough, go-it-alone, independent image of Texas and Houston is largely mythical. For Houston is highly dependent—so dependent, in fact, that it is in many ways an economic colony steered from elsewhere. Take, for example, energy products. Houston businesses, and their workers, are heavily dependent on energy markets whose prices are controlled in such places as New York and Saudi Arabia. This city's entrepreneurs and workers can be severely affected by a rise or fall in the market price of agricultural products or oil-gas products. Moreover, in contrast to Houston's image as the oil capital, no major oil company has its international headquarters there. And the new electronics and other high-tech industries that have emerged in the last three decades in Houston are for the most part dependent on outsiders as well—on investment decisions made in the offices of firms like IBM (New York) or Lockheed (Los Angeles) and on

the huge federal space contracts and medical research grants. Economic changes outside shape the Houston economy in fundamental ways.

Houstonians have long been proud of winning national independence at San Jacinto in 1836; they and their fellow Texans even put up a monument to that battle in the late 1930s. Yet that great monument to Texas independence was built with federal government money.

Diversity

Another view of Houston shown to be mythical in our analysis is its representation as a homogeneous and affluent city. In contrast to this picture, Houston is diverse in its class, occupational, racial, and ethnic composition. There are hundreds of distinctive residential areas in the metropolitan area, ranging from wealthy white communities to large moderate- and low-income white communities with high unemployment, to some of the oldest black communities in the Sunbelt. In recent decades the city's Hispanic communities have grown dramatically.

Chapter 4 described the diversity of neighborhoods in Houston and their efforts to define themselves as distinct communities within the city. The more than 500 citizens' groups in Houston attest to the existence of these distinct communities.

In addition to self-defined communities within Houston, residential segregation further defines distinctive Hispanic and black communities (Chapters 5 and 6). These can be distinguished not only by their racial and ethnic composition but also by the amenities and disamenities they receive. Some areas benefited more from Houston's growth (and suffered less from its decline) than others. The location of the city's garbage dumps in predominantly black neighborhoods and the differential provision of basic city services (e.g., running water) define these "privileged" and "neglected" areas.

Thus, the mosaic of communities that makes up Houston is more than a description of Houston's diversity; it is an indication of inequality. For even as Houston "boomed," sections of the city did not. Similarly, Houston's "bust" hurts some communities within the city more than others. To understand the city, one must look, as we have tried to do, at the diversity of communities that compose it.

Houston's Oil Pillar in Crisis

The base of the Houston economy is oil. But the oil economy has suffered a serious decline. In 1983 proven oil reserves in Texas totalled 7.6 billion barrels. That year oil was pumped out at 2.5 million barrels a day, or just under a billion barrels for the year. Proven oil reserves in Texas will be exhausted, at these pumping rates, in about seven to ten years if no new reserves are discovered. New reserves will doubtless be discovered but likely at a sharply declining rate. It is possible that the oil fields will be dormant in 20 to 30 years. And before all the oil is gone, the decline in oil pumped will have significant effects on the Texas and Houston economies. Optimistic oil experts note that high-tech recovery techniques can bring large pools of hard-to-get oil out of the ground. But at today's oil prices many technically possible recovery techniques are not feasible. Lower prices have the effect of reducing the rate at which oil is pumped out of the remaining fields. Lower prices also slow significantly the investment of time and money in drilling for new oil.

The Houston oil economy is not an island unto itself, nor is it simply part of a boom-bust Texas economy. It is a dependent part of a *world* economy. Oil-related jobs in Houston may gradually decline as the oil runs out. But jobs will decline even more precipitously as the price of OPEC oil drops. Work by Thomas Plaut at the Bureau of Business Research at the University of Texas suggests that a one-dollar-per-barrel drop in OPEC-shaped oil prices means a $3 billion drop in Texas economic output. A seven-dollar-per-barrel fall in the price of oil would reduce state economic output by an estimated $21 billion.[2] A change this large would mean the loss of many more jobs for Houstonians.

By the early 1980s parts of Texas, from Midland to Houston, were declining. There was an oil glut, and the price for a barrel of oil had fallen sharply. Around Texas employment in oil-field machinery firms dropped from 150,000 in 1981 to 75,000 in 1984, while employment in oil and gas extraction dropped from a bit more than 150,000 to about 135,000. Employment in oil refining dropped in the same period. In 1986 the Houston-area employment in oil-field service companies was still only about 50 percent of the 1981 peak of 47,900 workers.

The unemployment rate grew more rapidly in Houston than in the nation, hitting 9.7 percent in 1983 (more than 10 percent for two months), up sharply from 1981. Between 1982 and 1983 Houston lost just under 100,000 jobs. In 1983 Houston had 952 business failures with $3.8 billion in total assets, a substantial increase from 1982; in 1984 the number

of bankruptcies continued to skyrocket. In addition, there was a general decline in oil refinery use in Texas, from 91 percent of capacity in the late 1970s to less than 70 percent of capacity in 1983.[3]

Numerous drilling companies and other oil-field service firms went out of business in 1983–1984. With lower oil prices, less drilling, and fewer oil companies (the result of mergers), there are fewer customers for oil-field service companies. And with more oil companies putting money into debt retirement or into the omnipresent mergers, there is less money for oil drilling contracts. With the slump in demand for oil-field equipment, some individual companies "now have the capacity to serve the entire industry all by themselves."[4] Gas drilling, particularly onshore deep drilling, also dropped dramatically in 1983–1985, from 900 to 100 drilling rigs. This has significantly hurt workers in gas-related firms in Houston.

Beginning late in 1983 the oil industry in Houston began to recover from the severe recession of the previous year or so. Employment in the oil drilling and oil-field machinery areas improved somewhat between late 1983 and 1985, although not enough to restore employment to prerecession levels; this recovery was soon followed by yet another recession. It was not until late 1987 that Houston's economy stabilized somewhat, with an unemployment rate just under 8 percent.

Decline in the Oil and Petrochemical Arena: Industrial Houston

The Houston petrochemical industry, a very high-tech industry, faces serious problems. Third World countries such as Saudi Arabia, Mexico, and Nigeria are expanding their oil refining and petrochemical facilities in order to produce value-added products from their raw materials. Since the 1970s a number of large-capacity refineries have been started in Third World areas; much less capacity is being added in the United States. Major petrochemical complexes are being built in Saudi Arabia to sell products to Europe, thus reducing the market for Gulf Coast and other regional petrochemical products. The health of significant sectors of the Houston petrochemical economy currently depends on exports to other countries; yet some of these countries, including Mexico, are trying to decrease petrochemical imports and to build up their value-added, oil-related industries. These petrochemical industry trends pose major problems for workers in metropolitan Houston plants.

By the mid-1980s petrochemical demand was dropping and overcapacity

increasing. Over the last few decades petrochemical firms have been more concerned with what their competitors are doing than with the total market for petrochemicals. Vigorously competing with each other for market shares, they have created a situation in which overproduction results in recession, shutdowns, and cutbacks. New petrochemical plants are under construction in Canada, the Middle East, and elsewhere in the Third World. Since 1980 this worldwide overcapacity has forced European petrochemical manufacturers to shut down one-sixth of their capacity. In the United States cutbacks have also been implemented. In 1982, for example, the utilization rates in Diamond Shamrock's three large Houston petrochemical complexes fell to 60–65 percent, down from 90–95 percent just three years before. Exxon's Baytown plants also suffered dropping utilization rates; this reduction occurred just as a new plastics plant was opened. Several manufacturers, including Exxon, retired aging plants instead of spending capital to retool them. These cutbacks mean a loss of jobs.[5]

The petrochemical companies have mounted a reorganization strategy to meet the overproduction crisis. They are cutting capacity and retrenching in basic petrochemical production; they are concentrating more on producing higher-value specialty chemicals beyond the technological capacity of most Third World nations. This signals a structural realignment in the world petrochemical industry. A new two-tiered international division of labor in the petrochemical industry is emerging, which parallels tendencies at work in other U.S. manufacturing industries. Houston and other U.S. companies may gradually reduce major operations here, particularly for basic products like ethylene, and focus increasingly on specialty chemicals. Third World countries are expanding into basic petrochemical production. By 1985 the Saudi Arabian SABIC complex was expected to produce 2 million tons of ethylene annually, mostly for export at prices below those of western producers because of access to cheap raw materials.

Overseas expansion has involved U.S. petrochemical companies, which have participated in the overseas production in the form of joint ventures, a distinctive type of global sourcing. By providing technical and financial support to Third World projects, these U.S. companies get a stake in petrochemical business that competes with their own domestic operations in the metropolitan Houston area. In 1983 Diamond Shamrock, for example, owned a petrochemical plant in Chile and joint-venture plants in Brazil and in Korea. In 1983 Celanese had a plant in Mexico, while Exxon had plants in Scotland, Saudi Arabia, and Canada. Shell's largest chemical complex was in Saudi Arabia. U.S. jobs are lost in this fashion as U.S. oil and petrochemical companies engage in the global sourcing of petrochemicals.

This global sourcing means fewer jobs for Houston workers but more jobs for Third World workers, many of whom work for very low wages.

It is clear from the 1983–1986 decline in the price of many farm and ranch commodities that agriculture—also dependent on the world market—may not be positioned to make up for the long-term decline in other parts of the Houston economy. Houston was a major grain and cotton marketing center well before it became the "oil capital of the world."

The Human Toll of Growth and Decline

The seriousness of downturns in Houston's oil economy became especially clear when framed against the backdrop of the ideology of growth that has long characterized the city. In an article on Houston's demography, Roberto Marchesin and Joanne Austin argued that:

> Houstonians measure progress in terms of population increase, sur-
> face area extension, numbers of new buildings erected, and the con-
> tinual attraction of business to the area. They take great pride in
> Houston's rise to fifth largest city in the nation from fourteenth in
> 1950. They view the benefits of growth not only monetarily but also
> as a means of developing the arts, education, and medicine. In short,
> growth brings the good life, and, from the Houstonians' point of view,
> the good life keeps Houston growing.[6]

According to these researchers, Houston's growth is seen as favorable for the quality of life in Houston. Here Houstonians as a group are seen as measuring their progress in money and quality of life in terms of growth and development.

But in reality Houston has not been the utopia these views suggest. In the first place, Houston has a huge poor and moderate-income population that has yet to see the "good life" promised by rapid growth. Even for the more affluent middle- and upper-income Houstonians there are severe problems resulting from massive urban growth.

Sewage and Subsidence

Houston's growth has created many problems as the growth coalition seeks ever-increasing capital accumulation for the dominant business elite. Take, for example, the mundane problems of sewage disposal and safe water

supplies. Houston has a very serious sewage problem. In the early 1980s three-quarters of the city was under a sewer moratorium, that is, there was not enough sewage-treatment-plant capacity in many areas to permit any more sewer connections. So developers had to scramble, trading sewer rights with other developers, using permits they got before the moratorium, and switching permits from one area to another. Some developers built temporary sewage plants of their own, an expensive burden that the city government eventually will have to shoulder. This is particularly problematic in the scattered suburban developments just beyond the city limits, where there is sometimes heavy sewage discharge. As a consequence, there is great pressure on government to spend more for sewage facilities.[7]

One of the unusual consequences of development in Houston is subsidence, the gradual sinking of the city. Houston is 50 feet above sea level, and the heavy use of underground water there weakens the supporting soil structure. Together with oil and gas extraction and the weight of new development and construction, the dewatering of the soil has led to a drop in land elevation of several feet over the last seven decades. Numerous areas in central Houston are today four or five feet lower than they were in the early 1900s. Today it is estimated that most areas are sinking at a rate of one foot every five to six years. Subsidence creates serious flooding as well as construction and structural problems.[8]

Traffic Congestion

The most obvious problem of Houston's vigorous development is traffic. Houston has been famous for its over 200-mile freeway system, one of the largest in the world. Billions in planned freeway construction will eventually bring that up to 406 miles of 11 different freeways. According to a brochure put out by the Houston Chamber of Commerce, "any point in Houston can be reached within one hour" using this freeway system.[9] Reading chamber of commerce advertising such as this might lead one to think Houston has little or no transportation problem. That is not the case. By the 1970s and 1980s some of Houston's roads were congested all day long. Many commuters drive an hour and a half to two hours—one way. The city and county governments are unable to provide enough roads to keep up with rapid development.

Houstonians are more heavily dependent on automobiles than are residents of most cities, and the city's architecture reflects this dependence. As a recent analysis by the U.S. Department of Transportation put it: "The visual character of Houston is dominated by an expansive mixture of com-

mercial and residential elements that cater to the automobile, the principal mode of travel . . . [There is] the visual confusion that results from conflicts between building design, vehicle control mechanisms, vehicle movement, advertising and other elements of an active commercial society." [10]

Housing

As we discovered in Chapter 4, Houston's middle- and upper-income residents have not become agitated about their urban problems in general. For the most part, the few who do organize focus on problems only as they immediately affect them. In recent years Houston has seen a few citizens' groups pressing for cleaner air, more parks (though fourth in population size, Houston is about 100th among cities in park acreage), and better transportation. Today more people are at least talking about the quality of life in Houston.

Some of Houston's low- and moderate-income residents have paid a heavy displacement price for urban growth. Development in Houston has displaced some homeowners and tenants. If homeowners refuse to sell, developers can use a variety of tactics. They may start bulldozing the homes that they have title to (over 4,000 apartment units were leveled in 1986–1987), put up a multistory building, and watch the homeowners who refuse to sell suffer from the shade of the building, traffic flow, and noise. Eventually, these pressures force most people to sell. The most stubborn homeowners may simply see a development project built around them. In Houston one hotel was actually built around the home of a couple who refused to sell. [11]

It is Houston's low-income and minority homeowners and tenants who have suffered the most from market-oriented growth. In the western half of the central city, which is within "the loop," a major circumferential highway, black and Mexican-American low- and moderate-income families suffer from pollution and poor services and in some areas are under pressure from developers. A few pockets in the central city have suffered from significant racial gentrification, the replacement of poorer minority families with better-off professional, technical, and managerial (white) families who wish to live near their jobs in the office towers and office and medical parks. In a few small areas, land speculators are even buying up the oil leasing rights; there may be condominiums and oil wells next to one another in the inner city.

Minorities

As we noted previously, the Fourth Ward is one of Houston's large black communities with the misfortune of being near the central business district. The area is populated by predominantly black tenants living in single-family dwellings within a major public housing project. Because of its proximity to downtown, developers are eyeing the area. A number of prominent consultant reports have suggested that the area be redeveloped. While the consultant studies have noted the housing plight of black tenants, they offer no real solutions. Much of the Fourth Ward area is owned by a dozen or so absentee landlords, who in the 1980s have asked prices too high for the developers. But the area soon will be redeveloped. In general, Houston has serious housing problems for low-income and middle-income families, minority and white. There are simply not enough houses or multifamily units at reasonable rents to adequately house the burgeoning population.[12]

One-fifth of Houstonians live near or below the federal poverty line. Yet Houston has little public housing—only 5,000 units—and city planners show no interest in such construction. In 1980 there were 4,500 families and individuals on a waiting list for this housing. According to a Housing Authority planner, a lot of people are "living in cars," particularly near the public housing projects. Other poor are the homeless who live in or near the downtown area. Yet many powerful local officials scoff at the idea that Houston's poverty is of great consequence. A former mayor and chamber of commerce head, Louis Welch, put it this way in an interview with the *New York Times*: "The free market place has functioned in Houston like no other place in America. It has a method of purging itself of slums." Yet Houston has a serious problem in its inferior government services.

A Fiscal Crisis

By the 1980s Houston's newspapers were dramatizing the unprecedented fiscal crisis in the "shining buckle of the Sunbelt." In 1981 Houston's general-fund balance was $70 million; by fiscal year 1983 it slumped to a deficit of $43 million. The mid-1980s saw more red ink in the city's budget. The projected deficit for fiscal year 1989 is $55 million, and this comes on top of a 1988 deficit of $20 million. Like northern cities with fiscal crises, Houston finds itself with expenditures rising much more rapidly than tax revenues. Recent strategies to contain the deficit include limiting salaries and benefits of public employees (e.g., police officers). This tactic

has backfired in the case of police officers; in response to salary and benefit freezes the police force has limited the number of traffic citations it issues. In January 1988 only 41,000 tickets were issued, compared with the usual 100,000 per month. This of course adds to the deficit by reducing court revenues. One interesting aspect of Houston's recurring fiscal crisis is that it was not caused by factors alleged to be sources of fiscal crisis in northern cities, such as well-paid city workers.[13] Some observers have attributed the crisis to the oil-gas recession that hit Houston in 1982–1987. More basic reasons are closely tied to the costs of growth. In the mid-1980s Houston's city controller noted in a speech that Houston faced a gloomy fiscal picture, a retrenchment period with the possibility of service cutbacks.[14] In the 1970–1982 period Houston saw government revenues grow from $300 million to $2 billion. But in the 1977–1982 period revenue increases for the two major local taxes, property and sales tax, slowed considerably. In the same period, however, city government expenditures increased much more rapidly, with sewer expenditures going up 88 percent and airport expenditures rising by 160 percent. Infrastructure costs are rising because of rapid growth and the neglect of service infrastructure, the underbuilt and inadequately maintained facilities across the city. The minimal-government approach is no longer viable.[15]

In the decades prior to the mid-1970s the business elite and the city government it dominated were able to ignore the needs of inner-city minority communities. But in the 1970s the growing power of minority voters and civil rights litigation led to a more representative mayor and city council and thus to successful pressures from central-city residents to expand public services. The effective enfranchisement of minority voters has put increased pressure on the city government's budget.[16]

In addition, fiscal conservatism in Houston has resulted in a weak tax base for Houston's government. Property taxes, the major source of revenue, have declined. Moreover, in the past Houston relied on aggressive annexation of nearby areas to expand its tax base to cover city government and public services. Yet the cost of providing adequate services in annexed areas has reduced the utility of this strategy for raising revenues.[17]

Given this minimal-government approach, Houston has been unable to absorb its high velocity of investment and population growth without pain and crisis. Billions of dollars of investments since the 1940s have been channeled into oil refineries, petrochemical complexes, office towers, and shopping malls. This capital flow has generated a broad array of skilled and unskilled jobs and stimulated Houston's growth from a city of 385,000 in 1940 to a city of 1.7 million in the 1980s.

This sharp population increase has accelerated the city's infrastructure needs, particularly given the past underdevelopment and undermaintenance of the infrastructure and the laissez-faire approach to government. As a result, the *future* of the city's public services looks relatively bleak. Never very good in times of growth and prosperity, in times of economic downturn the services are even more deficient. Yet not all parts of the city suffer alike. Upper-income residential areas, shopping malls, and office-building projects pay extra to get the maintenance and security services they need; it is the poor and moderate-income Houstonians who suffer the most from a broad array of inadequate public services. If indeed the city faces a slow downward trend in its economy, the public service situation is likely only to worsen. The situation is so acute that Mayor Whitmire, long a foe of increased taxes, has proposed a 19 percent increase in the city property tax rate.

Before concluding this chapter, we turn briefly to some of the recent efforts to bring greater economic diversity to the "oil capital of the world."

Can a New Industry Bail Out the City?

Faced with a declining oil economy, some Houston business and political leaders have gone for what is called the high-tech solution. High-tech has come to mean the electronics/computer/defense industries. However, one should remember that Houston's oil refining and petrochemical production are old high-tech industries, in some ways (e.g., capital per worker) more technologically sophisticated than electronics production. The business elites in cities such as Houston and Dallas are aggressively seeking out high-technology firms, many of which are headquartered in cities far from Texas. Local city elites have courted the East Coast, West Coast, and Midwest electronics and computer companies.

Houston's Chamber of Commerce devised a new $5.5 million economic diversification push for the city. A February 1985 article in the chamber of commerce magazine, *Houston*, did not mention the oil industry as one of the city's attractions.[18] Rather, it targeted the new businesses needed to revitalize the Houston economy in this order: (1) biomedical research, (2) research and development laboratories, (3) instrument companies, (4) communications equipment firms, (5) inorganic chemical industries, (6) materials processing research, (7) office machines and computers, (8) engineering and architectural services, and (9) distribution services. The targets are service industries and a variety of high-tech firms. Hous-

ton's good business climate of low taxes, nonunion labor, and investment capital is cited by the local growth coalition as giving the city an edge in competing with other high-tech centers. Similarly, the Texas Economic Development Commission has published a booklet, *Texas, Space to Expand*, that is designed to attract high-tech industries. The first page and the governor's letter accompanying the booklet emphasize that Texas has the "most favorable business climate for new and expanding companies."

Yet high-tech electronics companies are not likely to bail the city of Houston out of its economic difficulties. Even as the city accelerated its economic diversification program, the semiconductor industry fell into a serious recession, with a large number of workers around the country suffering layoffs. It is ironic that just as Houston's growth coalition has come to recognize the need for economic diversity—and has sought out the electronics and other high-tech industries—other city growth coalitions have done the same thing. It is doubly ironic that an economic decline in some of those industries has paralleled Houston's efforts. Such conditions do not bode well for the future of Houston's economy.

Houston's Political Future

Before we leave this broad question of Houston's future, we can shift from economic questions to the political issues we explored in Chapters 2 and 3. In those chapters we illustrated the relatively modest role of local governments in Houston's past and present prosperity. Houston has perhaps the weakest local government of any major city in North America. There are no suburban governments of much significance; the outlying governments that are of significance are in relatively old, self-contained cities such as Pasadena and Baytown, areas that are not really suburbs.

The political history of Houston since 1910, contrary to its laissez-faire image, is a history of federal government intervention channeled and directed by the local business coalition. This growth coalition has frequently operated through the local government, as in the case of the infrastructure development funded by the federal government in the 1930s. But it has sometimes operated independently of that local government, as in the case of the recruitment of NASA to the Houston area. In the mid-1980s the Houston Chamber of Commerce functioned as a type of local government. (In fact, the president of the Houston Chamber of Commerce earns a higher salary than the mayor.) It commissioned many of the planning studies of Houston's social and economic problems, including an

important study on how to improve the economic diversity of the city. And the chamber has been active in setting up organizations to boost the city's economic image and to recruit new types of industry to diversify the city.

In 1985, moreover, some members of the chamber of commerce played a role in getting the chamber's head, former mayor Louis Welch, to run against the incumbent mayor, Kathy Whitmire. Welch lost in a close race, primarily because Houston's minority communities, particularly the black community, supported Whitmire. Whitmire's successful bids for mayor illustrate some of the recent changes in Houston. She was elected on a "fiscal management" platform and has criticized the old-guard Houston developers and business interests. Her tenure as mayor signals a shift in the power structure, at least in the sense that a new group of voters is having a say in local politics. Whitmire is a "business" mayor, but she has responded to minority interests more than previous mayors.

In contrast to cities like New York and Chicago, Houston has never had significant grass-roots (e.g., immigrant political "machine") input into its local politics. The local government since 1910 has been business domi-nated in its decisions in regard to most major political issues, ranging from low taxes to the absence of zoning mechanisms. The one major change in local politics came in the 1970s with the first significant voter input from Houston's black and Hispanic communities. Minority voters have generally voted for the more liberal of the business-oriented mayoral candidates, thereby increasing the flow of dollars and services to the de-prived minority communities. However, this change resulted from outside influences, notably court-ordered changes forced on the city's white estab-lishment by a suit undertaken by members of its minority communities. This is perhaps the most significant internal change in Houston's politics since 1910, but it has not yet altered the fundamentally business-oriented, weak-government structure of the city. Well below average in government-provided services such as park land, sewers, and fire protection, Houston is still ruled by the city's business elite, which places a "good business climate"—with its low taxes, industrial subsidies, and antiunion orienta-tion—ahead of an adequate array of government-provided services. The increased voice of minority voters in Houston has not altered this basic fact; it remains to be seen whether the growing minority population will develop into a more powerful political force in Houston politics.

For the time being, the political future of Houston is likely to be more of the same: more chamber of commerce and other business involvement; weak, underfunded, poorly staffed city government; federal aid dispro-portionately for business projects; emphasis on the good business climate

Notes

Chapter 1

1. "Texas," *Fortune* 20 (Dec. 1939): 87.
2. Quoted in Gene Burd, "The Selling of the Sunbelt," in David Perry and Alfred J. Watkins (eds.), *The Rise of the Sunbelt Cities* (Los Angeles: Sage, 1977), p. 139.
3. *Ibid.*
4. David G. McComb, *Houston: A History* (Austin: University of Texas Press, 1981), p. 192.
5. "A Texas City That's Busting Out All Over," *U.S. News & World Report* (Nov. 27, 1978): 47.
6. Quoted in McComb, *Houston*, p. 9.
7. *Ibid.*, pp. 9–10.
8. "New York Times Praises Houston," *Progressive Houston* 1 (Apr. 1909): 9.
9. P. W. Horn, quoted in *Progressive Houston* 1 (June 1909): 1–2.
10. Joseph A. Pratt, *The Growth of a Refining Region* (Greenwich, Conn.: JAI Press, 1980), pp. 23–24.
11. *Ibid.*, p. 29; McComb, *Houston*, p. 77.
12. Janet L. Abu-Lughod, *Cairo: 1001 Years of "The City Victorious"* (Princeton, N.J.: Princeton University Press, 1971), p. v.

Chapter 2

1. Most of the following chapter appeared in an earlier version. See Joe R. Feagin, "The Global Context of Metropolitan Growth: Houston and the Oil Industry," *American Journal of Sociology* 9 (1985): 1204–1230.
2. David McComb, *Houston: A History* (Austin: University of Texas Press, 1981).
3. Joseph A. Pratt, *The Growth of a Refining Region* (Greenwich, Conn.: JAI Press, 1980), pp. 53–56.
4. U.S. Department of Commerce, Bureau of the Census, *Historical Statistics of the United States* (Washington, D.C.: U.S. Government Printing Office, 1961), p. 462.
5. Harold F. Williamson *et al.*, *The American Petroleum Industry: The Age of Energy 1899–1959* (Evanston, Ill.: Northwestern University Press, 1963), p. 330.
6. Marquis James, *The Texaco Story* (New York: The Texas Company, 1953), pp. 60–73.
7. Henrietta M. Larson and Kenneth W. Porter, *History of Humble Oil and Refining Company* (New York: Harper and Row, 1959), pp. 72–73.
8. *Ibid.*, pp. 75–104.
9. McComb, *Houston*, pp. 80–81.
10. *Ibid.*, p. 85.
11. "Texas," *Fortune* 20 (1939): 85–95, 162.
12. Pratt, *The Growth of a Refining Region*, pp. 66–67.

13. Writers Program, Works Progress Administration, *Houston: A History and Guide* (Houston: Anson Jones Press, 1942), p. 120.

14. David Prindle, *Petroleum Politics and the Texas Railroad Commission* (Austin: University of Texas Press, 1981), pp. 35–40, 186–187.

15. James, *The Texaco Story*, p. 78.

16. Clarence H. Cramer, *American Enterprise* (Boston: Little, Brown, and Co., 1972), p. 279.

17. James, *The Texaco Story*, p. 77; Larson and Porter, *History of Humble Oil*, pp. 566–587.

18. Cramer, *American Enterprise*, p. 575.

19. Interview with J. L. Taylor, economic development officer, Houston Chamber of Commerce, July 1983.

20. James W. Lamare, *Texas Politics: Economics, Power, and Policy* (St. Paul, Minn.: West, 1981), pp. 15–16.

21. "Buildings for 100,000 Square Feet or More," *Houston* 52 (1981): 32–37.

22. Jack Donahue, *Big Town, Big Money* (Houston: Cordovan Press, 1973), pp. 48–50.

23. Joe R. Feagin, "The Secondary Circuit of Capital: Office Construction in Houston, Texas," *International Journal of Urban and Regional Research* (Spring 1987): 172–192.

24. Taylor interview.

25. Thomas R. Plaut, *Energy and the Texas Economy: Past, Present, and Future*, research report (Austin: Bureau of Business Research, University of Texas, 1982), p. 203.

26. Bronwyn Brock, "Houston Less Vulnerable than Dallas-Ft. Worth to Impact of the Recession," *Voice* (Dallas Federal Reserve Bank) (Oct. 1981): 1–3.

27. Texas Commerce Bancshares, *Texas Facts and Figures* (Houston: Economics Division, Texas Commerce Bancshares, Inc., 1982), pp. 24–25.

28. Robert Reinhold, "Prosperity of Texas Begins to Fade as Prices for Its Oil Treasure Fall," *New York Times*, Mar. 20, 1983.

29. Mickey Wright, *Texas Industrial Wateruse Long-Term Projection* (Austin: Texas Department of Water Resources, 1982), unpub. report.

30. Mark Gottdiener, *Planned Sprawl* (Beverly Hills, Calif.: Sage, 1977).

31. Pratt, *The Growth of a Refining Region*, p. 506.

32. Brian J. L. Berry, *Growth Centers in the American Urban System*, vol. 1 (Cambridge, Mass.: Ballinger, 1973).

Chapter 3

1. R. D. Norton, *City Life-Cycles and American Urban Policy* (New York: Academic Press, 1979), pp. 17–25.

2. *Ibid.*

3. Joseph Sikmund III, "A Theoretical Structure for the Study of Suburban Politics," *Annals* 422 (Nov. 1975): 45–60.

4. The extent of a Texas home-rule city's ETJ is based on its population. Cities of more than 100,000 have a five-mile reach. That reach is reduced as follows: 50,000 to 99,999—3.5 miles; 25,000 to 49,999—2.5 miles; 5,000 to 24,999—1 mile.

5. ACIR, *Regional Decision-Making: New Strategies for Substate Districts*. Vol. 1, *Substate Regionalism and the Federal System* (Washington, D.C.: U.S. Government Printing Office, 1973), p. 21.

6. For an extensive treatment of water districts in the Houston area, see Virginia Marion Perrenod, *Special Districts, Special Purposes: Fringe Governments and Urban Problems in the Houston Area* (College Station: Texas A&M University Press, 1984).

7. Data for Harris County water districts were obtained from the Texas Water Rights Commission.

8. Robert D. Thomas, "Metropolitan Structural Development: The Territorial Imperative," *Publius: The Journal of Federalism* 14 (Spring 1984): 83–115.

9. David G. McComb, *Houston: The Bayou City* (Austin: University of Texas Press, 1968), p. 94.

10. *Ibid.*, p. 174.

11. Deil Spencer Wright, *Understanding Intergovernmental Relations* (North Scituate, Mass.: Duxbury, 1978), pp. 45–49.

12. *Houston Post*, Dec. 8, 1940.

13. "114,000 Employed in Houston's Busy Industrial Plants," *Houston Magazine* (1943): 7–14.

14. Wright, *Understanding*, p. 49.

15. David Bradstreet Walker, *Toward a Functioning Federalism* (Cambridge, Mass.: Winthrop, 1981), pp. 65–95.

16. Jimmy Lowery, "An Investigation into Substandard Housing Conditions in Houston" (M.A. thesis, University of Houston, 1971).

17. Kenneth E. Gray, *A Report on the Politics of Houston* (Cambridge, Mass.: Joint Center for Urban Studies, MIT and Harvard, 1960), pp. 1–22.

18. *Ibid.*, p. vi–27.

19. *Houston Post*, Jan. 15, 1950.

20. McComb, *Houston*, pp. 170, 183.

21. Lowery, "An Investigation."

22. *Houston Post*, Aug. 30, 1975, reported that the ratio of need to available units in Houston was 10 to 1 and that no other city approached a ratio that low.

23. *Houston Post*, July 22, 1950.

24. *The Politics of Federal Grants* (Washington, D.C.: Congressional Quarterly Press, 1981), pp. 96–99.

25. Data for per capita federal aid and federal aid as a percentage of a city's own sources of revenue were collected for the 51 largest U.S. cities. These data include only direct receipts from the federal government. Indirect federal aid (state pass-throughs) is not appropriate to this analysis because these funds go almost entirely for welfare, highways, and education and thus go to special districts rather than cities.

26. Susan A. MacManus, *Federal Aid to Houston* (Washington, D.C.: The Brookings Institution, 1983), p. 14.

27. Robert D. Thomas, "Intergovernmental Coordination in the Implementation of National Air and Water Pollution Policies," in Charles O. Jones and Robert D. Thomas (eds.), *Public Policy Making in the Federal System* (Beverly Hills, Calif.: Sage, 1976), pp. 129–148.

28. MacManus, *Federal Aid*, pp. 41–46.

29. Many Hispanics have dropped the use of accents and tildes from their names; therefore, we use them only when the person cited uses them.

30. MacManus, *Federal Aid*, pp. 41–46.

31. *Ibid.*

Chapter 4

1. Susan A. MacManus, "Options for Managing Urban Growth: Citizen Perceptions and Preferences," Center for Public Policy, Discussion Paper Series, 1982, no. 83-3.

2. Unibook, Inc., *Houston, City of Destiny* (New York: Macmillan, 1980), p. 82.

3. Joe R. Feagin, "The State in the 'Free Enterprise' City: The Case of Houston," *Environment and Planning D: Society and Space* 2 (1984): 447–460.

4. Harold Platt, *City Building in the South* (Philadelphia: Temple University Press, 1983), p. 23.

5. MacManus, "Options."

6. John Mollenkopf, *The Contested City* (Princeton, N.J.: Princeton University Press, 1983), p. 106.

7. Marquis James, *The Texaco Story* (New York: The Texas Company, 1953), p. 78.

8. William D. Angel, Jr., "The Politics of Space: NASA's Decision to Locate the Manned Spacecraft Center in Houston," *The Houston Review*, vol. 6, no. 2 (1984).

9. Robert Fisher, *Let the People Decide* (Boston: G.K. Hall, 1984).

10. *Ibid.*

11. *Ibid.*

12. Angel, "The Politics of Space."

13. Fisher, *Let the People Decide*.

14. Joe R. Feagin and Beth Anne Shelton, "Community Organizing in Houston: Social Problems and Community Response," *Community Development Journal*, vol. 20, no. 2 (April 1985).

15. Manuel Castells, *The City and the Grassroots* (Berkeley: University of California Press, 1983).

16. Interview with Ann Lee, president of Braes Bayou Association, Houston, June 1984.

17. Interview with Roberta Burroughs, Assistant Director for Redevelopment, Department of Planning and Development, City of Houston, July 25, 1984.

18. Fisher, *Let the People Decide*; Burroughs interview; interview with Christine Stevens, The Metropolitan Organization, Houston, June 1984; interview with Judy Graves, Acorn official, Houston, May 1981; interview with Graves, Houston, 1984.

19. Burroughs interview, 1984.

20. Fisher, *Let the People Decide*.

21. Graves interview, May 1984; Stevens interview.

22. Interview with Ken Fujimoto, The Metropolitan Organization, Houston, June 1984; Stevens interview.

23. See also Fisher, *Let the People Decide*.

24. Graves interview, 1984.

25. *Ibid.*

26. *Ibid.*

27. *Ibid.*

28. Stephen Johnson, "Group Says Ethylene Smoke Caused Illness," *Houston Chronicle*, Jan. 28, 1983.

29. Stevens interview.

30. "Changing the Image," *Inner-View*, vol. 5, no. 1 (Jan. 1984); West Houston Activity Report, "West Houston Association—A Description," June 1984; City Post Oak Association, "Report to the Membership," Jan. 1985.

31. Patricia Stofer, personal correspondence with Beth Anne Shelton, Mar. 26, 1985.

32. *Ibid.*

33. "West Houston Association."

34. City Post Oak Association, "Report."

35. *Ibid.*

36. Bill Mintz, "Group Hopes to Revive 'Can do' Spirit Here," *Houston Chronicle*, Nov. 29, 1983.

37. *Inner-View*, "Changing the Image."

38. Houston Chamber of Commerce, "Civic Affairs Action Plan," 1981: 1.

39. Efraim Garcia, quoted in "A Fourth Ward Overview," *Cite* (Winter 1984): 12.

40. Gladys House, quoted in "A Fourth Ward Overview," 12.

41. Diane Y. Ghirardo, "Wielding the Hatchet at Allen Parkway Village," *Cite* (Winter 1984): 13–16.

42. Peter Saunders, *Social Theory and the Urban Question* (New York: Holmes and Meier, 1981); Castells, *The City*; Peter Saunders, "Beyond Housing Classes: The Sociological Significance of Private Property Rights in Means of Consumption," *International Journal of Urban and Regional Research*, vol. 8, no. 2 (1984).

43. Saunders, *Social Theory.*

44. Castells, *The City.*

Chapter 5

1. O. F. Allen, *The City of Houston from Wilderness to Wonder* (Temple, Tex.: O. Fisher Allen, 1936), p. 1.

2. Kenneth W. Wheeler, *To Wear a City's Crown* (Cambridge, Mass.: Harvard University Press, 1968), p. 109.

3. See Henry A. Bullock, *Pathways to the Houston Negro Market* (Ann Arbor, Mich.: J. N. Edwards, 1957); Henry A. Bullock, *Profile of the Negro Business Enterprises: A Survey and Directory of Their Attitudes* (Houston: Negro Chamber of Commerce, 1962).

4. See *Houston Informer*, June 14, 1919.

5. *Ibid.*

6. David G. McComb, *Houston: The Bayou City* (Austin: University of Texas Press, 1968), p. 157.

7. See Robert L. Lineberry, *Equality and Urban Policy: The Distribution of Municipal Public Service* (Beverly Hills, Calif.: Sage, 1977), ch. 1.

8. Kirkpatrick Sale, *Power Shift: The Rise of the Southern Rim and Its Challenge to the Eastern Establishment* (New York: Random House, 1975); G. Sternlieb and J. W. Hughes, *Post-Industrial America: Metropolitan Decline and Inner-Regional Jobs Shift*

(New Brunswick, N.J.: Rutgers University Center for Policy Research, 1975); David C. Perry and Alfred J. Watkins, *The Rise of the Sunbelt Cities* (Beverly Hills, Calif.: Sage, 1977).

9. U.S. Department of Housing and Urban Development, *Report of the President's Commission for a National Agenda for the Eighties* (Washington, D.C.: U.S. Government Printing Office, 1980), pp. 165–169.

10. U.S. Department of Commerce, Bureau of the Census, *State and Metropolitan Area Data Book 1982* (Washington, D.C.: U.S. Government Printing Office, 1982), p. 386. For an in-depth discussion of Houston's black community in the 1980s, see R. D. Bullard, *Invisible Houston: The Black Experience in Boom and Bust* (College Station: Texas A&M University Press, 1987).

11. See McComb, *Houston: The Bayou City*; David G. McComb, *Houston: A History* (Austin: University of Texas Press, 1981); Chandler Davidson, *Biracial Politics: Conflict and Coalition in the Metropolitan South* (Baton Rouge: Louisiana State University Press, 1972).

12. See R. D. Bullard, "Black Housing in the Golden Buckle of the Sunbelt," *Free Inquiry* 8 (Nov. 1980): 169–172.

13. David T. Wellman, *Portraits of White Racism* (Cambridge: Cambridge University Press, 1977), p. 37.

14. U.S. Bureau of the Census, *State and Metropolitan Area Data Book 1982*, p. 386.

15. Karl Taeuber, "Racial Residential Segregation, 28 Cities, 1970–1980," Center for Demography and Ecology, working paper no. 83-12, University of Wisconsin-Madison (March 1983), p. 3.

16. See Kathryn Nelson, *Recent Suburbanization of Blacks: How Much, Who and Where?* (Washington, D.C.: U.S. Department of Housing and Urban Development, 1979), p. 5; R. D. Bullard and O. L. Pierce, "Black Housing Patterns in a Southern Metropolis: Competition for Housing in a Shrinking Market," *The Black Scholar* 2 (Nov./Dec. 1979): 60–67; Larry Long and Deanna Deare, "The Suburbanization of Blacks," *American Demographics* 3 (Sept. 1981): 20; R. D. Bullard, "The Black Family: Housing Alternatives in the 80s," *Journal of Black Studies* 14 (Mar. 1984): 341–351.

17. William C. Hester, "Bordersville: Catching Up to the 21st Century," *Playsure Magazine* (Jan. 1980): 20; see also *Houston Post*, Dec. 13, 1981.

18. U.S. Bureau of the Census, *The Social and Economic Status of the Black Population in the United States: An Historical View, 1790–1978* (Washington, D.C.: U.S. Government Printing Office, 1979), p. 136.

19. William C. Matney and Dwight L. Johnson, *America's Black Population: 1970–1982* (Washington, D.C.: U.S. Government Printing Office, 1983), p. 23.

20. U.S. Bureau of the Census, *Provisional Estimates of Social, Economic, and Housing Characteristics* (Washington, D.C.: U.S. Government Printing Office, 1982), p. 110.

21. See Phillip L. Clay, *Neighborhood Revitalization: The Recent Experience in Large Metropolitan Cities* (Cambridge, Mass.: MIT Press, 1978); National Urban Coalition, *Displacement: City Neighborhoods in Transition* (Washington, D.C.: National Urban Coalition, 1978); S. Laska and D. Spain, *Back to the City* (New York: Pergamon Press, 1979); Howard J. Sumka, "Neighborhood Displacement and Revitalization," *Journal of the American Association of Planners* 45 (Oct. 1979): 480–487; Chester Hartman, D.

Keating, and R. Legates, *Displacement: How to Fight It* (Berkeley, Calif.: National Housing Law Project, 1982).

22. R. D. Bullard and D. L. Tryman, "Competition for Decent Housing: A Focus on Housing Discrimination Complaints in a Sunbelt City," *Journal of Ethnic Studies* 7 (Winter 1980): 52–63; R. D. Bullard and D. L. Tryman, *Economic Development Strategies for Houston's Fifth Ward: A Feasibility Study* (Houston: City of Houston, 1980); Housing Authority of the City of Houston, *Allen Parkway Village/Fourth Ward Technical Report*, 1983.

23. U.S. Department of Housing and Urban Development, *A New Partnership to Conserve America's Communities: A National Urban Policy Report* (Washington, D.C.: U.S. Government Printing Office, 1978), p. 69.

24. See J. Saltman, "Housing Discrimination: Policy, Research Methods, Results," *Annals of the Academy of Political and Social Sciences* 44 (Jan. 1979): 186–196.

25. U.S. Commission on Civil Rights, *The Federal Fair Housing Enforcement Effort: A Report of the U.S. Commission on Civil Rights* (Washington, D.C.: U.S. Government Printing Office, 1979).

26. Franklin Wilson, *Residential Consumption, Economic Opportunity, and Race* (New York: Academic Press, 1979), p. 108.

27. See Bullard and Tryman, "Competition for Decent Housing," pp. 51–63.

28. The Houston city attorney receives the housing discrimination complaints that the Fair Housing Division evaluates as having sufficient grounds for prosecution. However, only one housing discrimination case has reached the court in the history of the city's Fair Housing Division; this case was subsequently dismissed.

29. See Housing Authority of the City of Houston, *First Annual Report* (July 1940). This 32-page report illustrated the slum conditions in the city and included drawings of projects planned for the city. At the time over 25,680 families (or about 87,618 individuals) were living in substandard dwellings scattered across the city.

30. See *Houston Post*, Feb. 11, 1940; Housing Authority of the City of Houston, *Allen Parkway/Fourth Ward Technical Report*, 1983, p. ii–7.

31. Housing Authority of the City of Houston, *Annual Report of the Housing Authority of the City of Houston* (July 1984), p. 3.

32. Houston Community Development Office, *Community Development Program Application to the U.S. Department of Housing and Urban Development* (Houston: City of Houston, 1979).

33. Bullard and Pierce, "Black Housing Patterns," p. 65.

34. See Economic Research Associates, *Houston's Fourth Ward Study: Options Analysis* (Houston: City of Houston Economic Development Division, 1979), part 1; Housing Authority of the City of Houston, *Allen Parkway Village/Fourth Ward Technical Report*, 1983, ch. 5.

35. Edgar Shular, "The Houston Negro Riot," *Journal of Negro Education* 29 (1944): 300.

36. *Ibid.*, p. 321.

37. *Ibid.*, p. 322.

38. Robert V. Haynes, *A Night of Violence: The Houston Riot of 1917* (Baton Rouge: Louisiana State University Press, 1976), pp. 167–179.

39. John Hope Franklin, *From Slavery to Freedom: A History of Negro Americans* (New York: Alfred A. Knopf, 1974), p. 340.

40. *Ibid.*, p. 341.

41. Haynes, *A Night of Violence*, pp. 322–323.

42. National Advisory Commission on Civil Disorders, *Report of the National Advisory Commission on Civil Disorders* (New York: E. P. Dutton and Co., 1968), p. 41.

43. Chandler Davidson, *Biracial Politics*, pp. 84–85; *The Forward Times*, May 27, 1967; Bill Helmer, "Nightmare in Houston," *Texas Observer* (June 1967).

44. Davidson, *Biracial Politics*, p. 84.

45. Robert Hill, *The Widening Economic Gap* (Washington, D.C.: National Urban League, 1979); National Urban Coalition, *The Situation in Urban America: A Spring 1982 Report* (Washington, D.C.: National Urban Coalition, 1982); National Urban League, *The State of Black America* (Washington, D.C.: National Urban League, 1984).

46. U.S. Bureau of the Census, *1980 Census of Population and Housing*, Census Tracts, Houston, Texas SMSA, PHC80-2-184.

47. *Ibid.*

48. John Reid, "Black America in the 1980s," *Population Bulletin* 37 (Dec. 1982): 25; Matney and Johnson, *America's Black Population*, pp. 16–17.

49. Stephen L. Klineberg, "The Houston Area Survey—1985" (Rice University, Department of Sociology, March 1985).

50. *Ibid.*, pp. 130–133.

51. U.S. Department of Labor, *Geographic Profile of Employment and Unemployment* (Washington, D.C.: U.S. Government Printing Office, 1983, 1984).

52. Houston United Way, *Employment 1982: Report of the Priority Review Committee* (Houston: Houston United Way, 1982), pp. 26–27.

53. U.S. Bureau of the Census, *U.S. Census of Population*, Tables 129 and 135 (Washington, D.C.: U.S. Government Printing Office, 1983).

54. U.S. Bureau of the Census, *Advanced Estimates of Social, Economic, and Housing Characteristics: Texas* (Washington, D.C.: U.S. Government Printing Office, 1983), p. 145.

55. See William J. Wilson, *The Declining Significance of Race: Blacks and the Changing American Institutions* (Chicago: University of Chicago Press, 1978); James E. Blackwell and Phillip S. Hart, *Cities, Suburbs and Blacks* (Bayside, N.Y.: General Hall, Inc., 1983); Charles V. Willie, *Race, Ethnicity, and Socioeconomic Status* (Bayside, N.Y.: General Hall, Inc., 1983).

56. Joel Popkins, *Measuring Gross National Product Estimates: 1955–1976* (Washington, D.C.: U.S. Small Business Administration, 1980); White House Commission on Small Businesses, *America's Small Business Economy* (Washington, D.C.: U.S. Government Printing Office, 1980).

57. David L. Birch, *The Job Generation Process* (Washington, D.C.: Economic Development Administration, 1979).

58. Minority Business Development Agency, *Minority Business Enterprises Today: Problems and Their Causes* (Washington, D.C.: Minority Business Development Agency, 1982), pp. 2–15.

59. U.S. Department of Commerce, *1982 Survey of Minority-Owned Business Enterprises: Blacks* (Washington, D.C.: U.S. Government Printing Office, 1982), p. 87.

60. "The Top 100 Black Enterprises," *Black Enterprise* 13 (June 1984): 109–110.

61. *Ibid.*, p. 101.

62. Bullock, *Pathways*, pp. 60–63.

63. See F. H. Buttel and W. L. Flinn, "Social Class and Mass Environmental Beliefs: A Reconsideration," *Environment and Behavior* 10 (Sept. 1978): 433–450; L. Tucker, "The Environmentally Concerned Citizen: Some Correlates," *Environment and Behavior* 10 (Sept. 1978): 389–418; Susan C. Cutter, "Community Concern: Social and Environmental Influences," *Environment and Behavior* 13 (Jan. 1981): 105–124; R. D. Bullard, "Solid Waste Sites and the Black Houston Community," *Sociological Inquiry* 53 (Spring 1983): 273–288.

64. Constance Perrin, *Everything in Its Place: Social Order and Land Use in America* (Princeton, N.J.: Princeton University Press, 1977); R. D. Bullard and B. H. Wright, "The Politics of Pollution: Implications for the Black Community," *Phylon* 47 (Mar. 1986): 71–78.

65. Ann B. Shlay and Peter H. Rossi, "Keeping up the Neighborhood: Estimating the Effect of Zoning," *American Sociological Review* 46 (Dec. 1981): 703–719.

66. David M. Smith, "Who Gets What Where and How: A Welfare Focus for Human Geography," *Geography* 59 (Nov. 1974): 289–297.

67. See Davidson, *Biracial Politics*; McComb, *Houston: A History*.

68. R. D. Bullard, "Endangered Environs: The Price of Unplanned Growth in Boomtown Houston," *California Sociologist* 7 (Summer 1984): 84–102.

69. Bullard, "Solid Waste Sites," p. 285.

Chapter 6

1. For an analysis of the global context of Houston's metropolitan growth, see Joe R. Feagin, "The Global Context of Metropolitan Growth: Houston and the Oil Industry," *American Journal of Sociology*, vol. 90, no. 6 (May 1985): 1204–1230.

2. The term *Hispanic* is used to mean the Spanish-origin, Spanish-surname, and/ or Spanish-language population. In the Houston metropolis this population is 88 percent Mexican in origin, mainly Mexican-American. In referring to the Spanish-origin population in the United States, it is impossible to find a term acceptable to all. Among the most commonly used are *Latino* and *Hispanic*. We use the latter term in this chapter because we sense it to be used more often than the former in the Houston area. In actuality, the majority of the Hispanics, that is, the Chicanos/Mexicanos, in the Houston area do not use this (English) term. Instead, they refer (in Spanish) to the person's nationality (e.g., "Juan, un Salvadoreño, . . ."). The issue of the proper term is significant, not merely academic; it reflects the sociocultural dynamism of "la gente."

3. F. Arturo Rosales, "Mexicans in Houston: The Struggle to Survive," *Houston Review*, vol. 3, no. 2 (1981): 249–252.

4. Interview with Dr. Thomas Kreneck, Houston Metropolitan Research Center, Houston, July 2, 1985.

5. Margarita Melville, *Mexicans in Houston* (Houston: Center for the Humanities, National Endowment for the Humanities, 1982), pp. 2–4.

6. Rosales, "Mexicans in Houston," pp. 250–254.

7. *Ibid.*

8. Mary Ellen Goodman, *The Mexican-American Population of Houston: A Survey in the Field 1965–1970* (Rice University Studies, vol. 57, no. 3, 1971), ch. 1.

9. Rodolfo Acuna, *Occupied America: A History of Chicanos* (New York: Harper & Row, 1981).

10. Interview with Dr. Thomas Kreneck, Houston Metropolitan Research Center, Houston, Texas, July 2, 1985.

11. Don Des Jarlais and Mary Ellen Goodman, *Houstonians of Mexican Ancestry* (Rice University, Center for Research and Social Change and Economic Development, 1968); Rosales, "Mexicans in Houston"; Melville, *Mexicans in Houston*.

12. Joe R. Feagin, "The Global Context of Metropolitan Growth: Houston and the Oil Industry," *American Journal of Sociology* 9 (1985): 1204–1230.

13. *Ibid.*, pp. 1213–1220; Houston Economic Development Council, "Houston Works for Business, Carry the Word," *Houston Chronicle*, Jan. 15, 1985.

14. "Power, Politics and the Shape of the City Council," *Houston Chronicle*, July 8, 1979.

15. "9-5 Council Plan Passes Easily," *Houston Post*, Aug. 12, 1979.

16. Don E. Carleton, *Red Scare! Right-wing Hysteria: Fifties Fanaticism and Their Legacy in Texas* (Austin: Texas Monthly Press), pp. 164–165.

17. *Ibid.*

18. "Houston's Spanish Accent Gets More Pronounced," *New York Times*, June 10, 1985.

19. Figures for the "white" category are estimates obtained by subtracting the Spanish-language or -surname (for 1970) and the Spanish-origin (for 1980) population from the census's white population. For 1980 people of Spanish origin who gave a self-identification as white were subtracted.

20. Feagin, "The Global Context of Metropolitan Growth," pp. 1211–1212.

21. Saskia Sassen-Koob, "The New Labor Demand in Global Cities," in Michael Peter Smith (ed.), *Cities in Transformation* (Beverly Hills, Calif.: Sage, 1984), pp. 139–171.

22. *Ibid.*, pp. 158–160.

23. "After Oil Bust, Better Times Ahead," *Houston Chronicle*, June 2, 1985.

24. *Ibid.*

25. Gilbert Cardenas and Estevan T. Flores, "Social, Economic and Demographic Characteristics of Undocumented Mexicans in the Houston Labor Market: A Preliminary Report" (Houston: Gulf Coast Legal Foundation, 1980).

26. Sassen-Koob, "The New Labor Demand," pp. 146–152.

27. *Ibid.*, p. 157.

28. The 33 percent rate for Hispanics in 1930–1940 is an estimate. We give this low estimate taking into consideration the decrease in immigration because of the depression and because of government roundup of Mexican immigrants. It is possible that for some years in this decade there was a net out-migration of Mexicans in the Houston area.

29. For immigration of Europeans, see Philip Taylor, *The Distant Mirror: European Emigration to the U.S.* (New York: Harper and Row, 1971).

30. Lawrence A. Cardoso, *Mexican Emigration to the United States, 1897–1931* (Tucson: University of Arizona Press, 1980).

31. Mario Barrera, *Race and Class in the Southwest: A Theory of Racial Inequality* (South Bend, Ind.: Notre Dame University Press, 1979), ch. 3.

32. Lance E. Davies and Robert E. Gallman, "Capital Formation in the United States during the Nineteenth Century," *The Cambridge Economic History of Europe*, Vol. 7, *The Industrial Economies: Capital, Labour, and Enterprise*, Part 2, Peter Mathias, ed. (Cambridge: Cambridge University Press, 1978).

33. Joe R. Feagin, *Racial and Ethnic Relations* (Englewood Cliffs, N.J.: Prentice-Hall, 1978), pp. 289–290.

34. Cardoso, *Mexican Emigration*, pp. 1–5.

35. *Ibid.*, p. 5.

36. Richard B. Craig, *The Bracero Program* (Austin: University of Texas Press, 1971).

37. Manuel García y Griego, "The Importation of Mexican Contract Laborers to the United States, 1942–1964." Working paper in U.S.-Mexican Studies, 11 (University of California, San Diego, Program in United States-Mexican Studies, 1980), p. 15.

38. "Employment of Mexican Nationals," Galveston, Texas, Oct. 27, 1944. This Sante Fe Railroad memorandum is located in the Santa Fe box in the archives at the Houston Metropolitan Research Center in the Houston Public Library.

39. Western Association of Railroad Executives, "Hints on the Employment of Imported Mexican Laborers," p. 4. See note 38 for location of document.

40. See Barrera, *Race and Class in the Southwest*, p. 122.

41. García y Griego, "The Importation of Mexican Contract Laborers," pp. 25–28.

42. W. A. Cornelius, L. R. Chavez, and J. G. Castro, *Mexican Immigrants and Southern California: A Survey of Current Knowledge* (San Diego, University of California, Program in United States-Mexican Studies, 1982), p. 32.

43. For a discussion of the European case, see Manuel Castells, "Immigrant Workers and Class Struggles in Advanced Capitalism: The Western European Experience," *Politics and Society* 5:1 (1975): 33–66.

44. M. Burawoy, "The Functions and Reproduction of Migrant Labor: Comparative Materials from South Africa and the United States," *American Journal of Sociology* 81 (Mar. 1976): 1057–1087.

45. "From El Salvador to Houston," *Texas Catholic Herald*, Jan. 13, 1984.

46. Frank D. Bean et al., *Estimates of the Number of Illegal Migrants in the State of Texas*, Texas Population Research Center Paper No. 4.001 (Austin: University of Texas, 1982).

47. Harley L. Browning and Ruth M. Cullen, "The Complex Formation of the Mexican-Origin Population" (University of Texas at Austin, Population Research Center, 1982), pp. 10–11. (Revised version of paper presented at the Conference on the Effects of Mexican Immigration on Mexican Americans, University of Texas at Austin, Oct. 22–23, 1982.)

48. Cardenas and Flores, "Social, Economic and Demographic Characteristics of Undocumented Mexicans"; Margarita B. Melville, "Selective Acculturation of Female Mexican Migrants," in Margarita B. Melville (ed.), *Twice A Minority: Mexican American Women* (St. Louis: The V. C. Mosby Company, 1980), pp. 155–163.

49. Cornelius, Chavez, and Castro, *Mexican Immigrants and Southern California*, pp. 17–19.

50. *Ibid.*

51. Cardenas and Flores, "Social, Economic and Demographic Characteristics of Undocumented Mexicans."

52. "Thousands Flock Here in Search of New Lives," *Houston Chronicle*, Sept. 23, 1984.

53. "From El Salvador to Houston," *Texas Catholic Herald*, Jan. 13, 1984.

54. *Ibid.*

55. "The Frustrating Fight of the Durans," *Houston Chronicle*, Sept. 23, 1984.

56. "Like All Immigrants, Salvadorans Import Culture and Customs," *Houston Chronicle*, Sept. 23, 1984.

57. *Ibid.*

58. "From El Salvador to Houston," *Texas Catholic Herald*, Jan. 13, 1984.

59. " 'Many of Us Have to Run, We Have No Choice'," *Houston Chronicle*, Sept. 23, 1984.

60. Director Paul B. O'Neill, Immigration and Naturalization Service, Houston Office. Immigration Forum, University of Houston-University Park, Apr. 2, 1985.

61. "From El Salvador to Houston."

62. "Illegal Aliens Taking Building Jobs Away from Texans, Officials Charge," *Houston Chronicle*, June 6, 1985.

63. The figures for the white category are derived by subtracting from the white category in the census the people of Spanish origin who gave a self-identification as white.

64. H. L. Browning and N. P. Rodriguez, "The Migration of Mexican Indocumentados as a Settlement Process: Implications for Work," in G. Borgas and M. Tienda (eds.), *Hispanics in the U.S. Economy* (New York: Academic Press, 1985).

65. U.S. Bureau of the Census, *1980 Census of Population and Housing*, Census Tracts, Houston, Texas, SMSA, PHC80-2-184.

66. For English industrial districts, see Arthur Redford, *Labour Migration in England, 1800–1850* (New York: Augustas M. Kelley, 1968), ch. 3.

67. "Big Acquisition Spurs Ethnic Mix at Houston Safeways," *Supermarket News* (Jan. 7, 1985): 20.

68. "Greed: The Rise and Fall of Lamar Terrace," *Houston City* (July 1985): 55.

69. Currently, there are plans to "redevelop" a low-income black residential district immediately west of downtown (the Fourth Ward). It is clear that the city and developers plan to bring a higher-income group into this area.

70. Browning and Rodriguez, "The Migration of Mexican Indocumentos as a Settlement Process."

71. See U.S. Bureau of the Census, *1980 Census of Population and Housing*, Census Tracts, Houston, Texas, SMSA, PHC80-2-184, Table p-20.

72. *Ibid.*

73. *Ibid.*

74. See U.S. Bureau of the Census, *1980 Census of Population and Housing*, Census Tracts, Houston, Texas, SMSA, PHC80-2-184, Table p-7. Rosenberg is the suburb with the highest proportion (40 percent) of Hispanics.

75. See U.S. Bureau of the Census, *1980 Census of Population and Housing*, Census Tracts, Houston, Texas, SMSA, PHC80-2-184, Table p-21. Rosenberg's median family income of $14,065 for Hispanics is the lowest for Hispanics in the Houston suburbs.

76. The native-born rate of the Houston Hispanic suburban population is 79 percent, 11 percentage points higher than the native-born rate in the central city. Rosenberg's rate of 83 percent is the highest of Hispanic populations in the suburbs. See U.S. Bureau of the Census, *1980 Census of Population and Housing*, Census Tracts, Houston, Texas, SMSA, PHC80-2-184, Table p-20.

77. Mexican-Americans constitute 85 percent of the Spanish-origin population in the city of Houston. In the suburbs with large Hispanic populations, Mexican-Americans

constitute the following proportions: Rosenberg, 95 percent; Baytown, 94 percent; Galena Park, 94 percent; Freeport City, 93 percent; Pasadena, 88 percent. See U.S. Bureau of the Census, *1980 Census of Population and Housing*, Census Tracts, Houston, Texas, SMSA, PHC80-2-184, Table p-7.

78. See U.S. Bureau of the Census, *1980 Census of Population and Housing*, Census Tracts, Houston, Texas, SMSA, PHC80-2-184, Table p-20.

79. Even during the depression Houston had substantial economic growth; see Feagin, "The Global Context of Metropolitan Growth," pp. 1214–1215. See also Richard Murray, "Houston: Politics of a Boomtown," *Dissent* (Fall 1980): 500.

80. Dr. Stephen L. Klineberg, "The Houston Area Survey—1985" (Rice University, Department of Sociology, March 1985).

81. Figures for the white category are estimates and include some people of Spanish origin. However, the true percentages for this category should not differ by more than two points from the figures in the table.

82. Cardenas and Flores, "Social, Economic and Demographic Characteristics of Undocumented Mexicans."

83. Gilbert Cardenas, "Manpower Impact and Problems of Mexican Illegal Aliens in an Urban Labor Market" (Ph.D. diss., Institute of Labor and Industrial Relations, University of Illinois at Urbana-Champaign, 1977).

84. U.S. Bureau of the Census, *1980 Census of Population and Housing*, Census Tracts, Houston, Texas, SMSA, PHC80-2-184.

85. *Ibid.*

86. Klineberg, "The Houston Area Survey—1985," Table 1.

87. "What Welfare Reform Did to the Working Poor," *Business Week* (June 17, 1985): 26.

88. *Ibid.*

89. U.S. Bureau of the Census, *1980 Census of Population and Housing*, Census Tracts, Houston, Texas, SMSA, PHC80-2-184.

90. "Panel Hits Schooling of Hispanic Youths," *Houston Chronicle*, Dec. 13, 1984.

91. Interview with Tina Reyes, school board member, Houston independent school district, Houston, Tex., July 1, 1985.

92. Interview of María Sáenz, Houston, Tex., Jan. 22, 1986.

93. Interview with Leonel Castillo, Houston International University, Houston, Oct. 3, 1984.

94. "The Hispanic Business 500," *Hispanic Business* (June 1985): 28–50.

95. "Service Industries Generating New Jobs," *Houston Chronicle*, June 23, 1985.

Chapter 7

1. T. R. Fehrenbach, *Seven Keys to Texas* (El Paso: Texas Western Press, 1983), pp. 1–40. For a more extended discussion of these issues, see Joe R. Feagin and Robert Parker, "Can Boom Turn to Bust?" *Texas Humanist* (May–June 1985): 1–7.

2. Thomas Plaut, "The Texas Economy: Current Status and Short-Term Outlook," *Texas Business Review* (Jan.–Feb. 1983): 15–20.

3. These statistics are largely drawn from 1983–1985 issues of the *Houston Business Journal*.

4. "Slump in Oilfield Equipment," *Houston Business Journal*, Mar. 11, 1985.

5. Interview with William Hoffman, Texas Department of Water Resources, 1983.

6. Roberto Marchesini and Joanne Austin, "Houston: Growth Center of the Southwest," *Texas Business Review* 52 (Aug. 1978): 164.

7. Patricia Cronkright, "Houston's Sewer Moratorium: Putting the Squeeze on Growth," *Houston Business Journal*, Dec. 18, 1980.

8. U.S. Department of Transportation, *Environmental Impact Statement* (Washington, D.C.: U.S. Government Printing Office, 1979), p. iii–56.

9. Houston Chamber of Commerce, "Houston Data Sketch," 1981 data sheet, in author's files.

10. U.S. Department of Transportation, *Environmental Impact Statement*, p. iii–58.

11. Interview with Patricia Cronkright, reporter for *Houston Business Journal*, Houston, May 1981.

12. Interview with Judy Graves, ACORN official, Houston, May 1981; interview with senior research official, Rice Center, Greenway Plaza, Houston, May 1981.

13. D. Bryant, "City in the Red," *Houston Business Journal*, Mar. 21, 1983.

14. M. Snyder, "Labor Says City Facing 'Retrenchment'," *Houston Chronicle*, Feb. 23, 1983.

15. Robert D. Bullard, "Solid Waste Sites and the Black Houston Community" (Paper presented at the annual meeting of the Southwestern Sociological Association, San Antonio, Mar. 17–20, 1982).

16. Susan A. McManus, *Federal Aid to Houston* (Washington, D.C.: Brookings Institution, 1983), p. 59.

17. Virginia M. Pevreuod, *Special Districts, Special Purposes: Fringe Governments and Urban Problems* (College Station: Texas A&M Press, 1984).

18. "Development Council Maps Economic Strategy," *Houston* (Feb. 1985): 9–14.

Index

Abu-Lughod, Janet, 7
ACORN, 61–62
Acres Home (Houston), 76
Advertisement, 5
Allen, Augustus and John, 5
Allen Parkway Village, 62, 67, 81; Residents' Council, 67–68
Allied Civic Clubs (ACC), 58–59
Aluminum, 18
Amoco, 19
Annexation, 10, 32, 35; and tax base, 36; and water districts, 35–36
Asians, 6
Astroworld, 7
Automobile, 12; production, 12

Ball, U.S. Rep. Thomas, 43
Banks, 11
Bayou City (Houston), 74
Baytown (Houston), 17, 32, 111
Beaumont, 11
Bilingual teacher, 117
Black, 8; business center, 71; businesses, 87; citizens, 71; community, 6, 48, 70, 74–75; earnings, 84; education, 84–85; neighborhoods, 49, 75–78; population growth, 75, 77; protestors, 83; suburbanization, 76; -white income gap, 84; work force, 14; workers, 71
Blacks, 4
Blue-collar work force, 14, 20
Bordersville (Houston), 76, 77
Bracero program, 102–103
Brazos River, 42
British-Dutch Shell Oil, 19
Brown, Lee, 84
Buffalo Bayou, 42
Business: activity centers, 22; associations, 64–67; leaders, 52–53; organization, 69
Butler, Asberry, 38

Cairo, Egypt, 7
Camp Logan, 82–83
Capital: flow during 1970s, 4; flow during World War II, 57

Capitalists, 4
Carvercrest (Houston), 76
Carverdale (Houston), 76
Catholic Church, 61
Central America, 8
Central American immigrants, 98, 104–105, 106
Central Business District, 67, 75
Central-city, 76; communities, 78
Central Houston Incorporated, 67
Chevron, 19
Chicago, IL., 20
Citizens': group, 53, 66; organization, 8
Citizens' Coalition for Responsive Government, 96–97
Citizens' Environmental Coalition, 63
City: attorney, 40; controller, 36, 39–40; council, 36, 38–39, 97; manager system, 37–38; services, 66; treasury, 40
City of Houston Department of Planning and Development, 64, 68; Neighborhood Revitalization Office, 60
City Post Oak Association (CPOA), 65
Civic: associations, 56, 59, 61, 89; clubs in post–World War II period, 58–60
Civil: lawsuits, 58; service system, 40
Class interests, 69
Cleveland, OH., 23
Coal, 12
"Collective-consumption" issues, 61, 63–64
Commercial capitalism, 11
Commercial center, 5
Commission, form of government, 36–37
Communities, 4, 6; black, 38, 75; Hispanic, 38 (see also Hispanic community)
Community: development, 53; groups, 55; organization, 55
Community-based: movement, 66, 69; movements' conflict with business organizations, 66–68
Community Development Block Grant, 91
Community development federal funds, 53
Competitive-industrial capitalism, 11–12, 71

Comprehensive Employment and Training Act (CETA), 47, 53
Conoco, 19
Construction, 18
Consumption: patterns, 69; sector interests, 69
Corporate investments, 12–13
Cotton, 11; brokerage companies, 11; center, 5–6, 26
Cultural identity goals, 60

Dallas, TX., 14
Decline, 23
Deed: enforcement of restrictions, 58; violations, 58
Demographers, 22
Detroit, MI., 9, 12, 21, 27
Development, 8, 9, 26, 57; control of, 59; of infrastructure, 15, 57; periods of, 10–28
Discrimination, 8, 71
Displacement, 78
Dowling Street Shootout, 83

East Texas oil fields, 9, 14–16
Economic downturn, 25
Economy, diversification of, 24
Educational: gap, 116; inequality, 116; level, 116
El Mercado commercial development, 61
El Mercado del Sol (Houston), 121
El Segundo Barrio (Houston), 94
Employment status, 113, 114
Environmental: organizations, 63–64; problems, 88
Expansion, 21
Exports, 4
Extraterritorial jurisdiction (ETJ), 7, 30, 32
Exxon, 19

FM 1960, 77
Fair Housing Division, 78
Fair Housing Ordinance, 78
Federal: aid, 15, 41–50, 50–52; dollars, 46; expenditures, 15–16
Federal Fair Housing Act of 1968, 78
Federal Voting Rights Act of 1965, 38
Federalism: grass-roots, 7, 41–44; regulatory, 7, 50–52, 78; selected advocacy, 7, 44–47
Fiesta stores, 119

Fifth Ward (Houston), 73, 78, 87
Fiscal crisis, 131–133
Ford, 9
Fortune, 3, 9, 15
Fourth Ward (Houston), 67, 71, 78, 81; control over, 68
Freedman's Town, 71; Association, 67, 68
Frenchy's Po-Boy, 87
Freeport City (Houston), 111
Freeport, TX., 44, 111
Fresh water supply districts (FWSDs), 35–36
Frostbelt, 23
Fuel oil, 12

Galena Park (Houston), 111
Garbage dumps, 90–91
Garcia, Efraim, 53
Garner, John Nance, 15
General Motors, 9
Gentrification, 23
"Golden Triangle", 44
Government: assistance, 42; during the 1930s, 7, 15–17; intervention during the 1940s, 16–17; structures, 36–41
Grains, 11
Grass Roots Federalism, 41–44
Graves, Curtis, 38
Graves, Judy, 62
Great Depression, 9, 13
Greenway Plaza (Houston), 23, 55
Gross National Product (GNP), 25
Growth, 3, 27; coalition, 5, 11, 14, 18, 22, 26, 28, 57; decentralized, 21–23; economic, 12–20; in the 1970s, 3–4; in the nineteenth century, 5–6; -pole theory, 11
Gulf, 19; Gulf Company, 11
Gulf Coast (Texas), 4, 9, 15, 18; refineries, 15

Hamilton, Carl, 83
Harris County, TX., 14, 30, 32, 34–35; Commissioner, 34
"Heavenly Houston", 73, 74
Hedwig Village (Houston), 112
Highway funds, 21
Highways, 21–22
Hispanic: American, 8; citizens, 71; community, 70; community development, 94, 107–113, 118–119, 120–122; immigrants, 94–95, 101; population growth,

96–97, 101, 107–108, 118–119; suburban growth, 111–113; transition zones, 109–110; work force, 114; zones, 108–111
Hispanicization, 109–110, 119–120
Hobby Airport (Houston), 46
Hofheinz, Mayor Fred, 50, 53
Holcombe, Oscar, 38, 48
Home ownership, 77, 78
Homesteading, 61
Housing, assistance, 80; condition, 130; private, 77
Housing Authority of the City of Houston (HACH), 48, 67 (*see also* Houston Housing Authority)
Houston: decline, 85; economy, 85, 86, 99, 100, 125–128; economic growth, 85; growth, 10, 26; police, 82, 84; population, 9; population growth, 9–10; redevelopment, 85; ship channel, 57; unemployment, 85
Houston Chamber of Commerce, 28, 49, 53, 133–134; Action Plan, 66
Houston Citizen Chamber of Commerce, 87
Houston City Council, 38, 42, 43
Houston District Navigation Company, 43
Houston Housing Authority, 62, 80
Houston Informer, 73
Houston Navigation District, 43
Houston Police Department, 62
Houston Post, 3
"Houston Proud", 66
Houston race riot of 1917, 82
Houston Traffic and Transportation Department, 65
Humble, 11; Baytown refinery, 17; Oil Company, 13, 17, 18
Hunters' Creek Village (Houston), 112

Image-building association, 65–66
Immigrant: Mexican population, 93, 101–102; undocumented workers, 8, 70; workers, 94, 103–104, 105–106
Income: difference, 112, 115–116; inequality, 112
Indochinese, 82
Indonesia, 24
Infrastructure, 18, 26, 41
Inner-city residents, 75
Intercontinental Airport, 46, 77
Investment, capital, 18

Jacinto City (Houston), 111
Jim Crow laws, 73, 95
Johnson, Lyndon B., 57
Johnson Space Center, 7
Jones, Jesse, 15
Jordan, Barbara, 38
"Juneteenth", 71

Land: -use, 88; use zoning, 88
Landlords, 78
Latin America, 25
League of United Latin American Citizens (LULAC): Council #60, 95; women's group, 95
Local: business, 29; business control, 52
Lopez, David T., 97
Los Angeles, CA., 21
Louisiana, 15
Low-income neighborhood, 79
Low-rent housing program, 79, 80–81
Low-wage work, 70
Lumber, 6, 11, 26
Lyon Avenue Commercial Corridor, 73

MacGregor neighborhood, 73
MacManus, Susan, 53
Magnolia barrio (Houston), 94
"Magnolia City" (Houston), 74
Malaysia, 24
Manufacturing, 5–6; center, 20–21; plants, 13–14
Mayor, 36–39; constraints on, 39–41
Mayor's Advisory Committee on Houston, 48
Mayor's Urban Redevelopment Committee, 46
Media, black, 74
Metal fabrication, 18
Metropolitan Organization, The (TMO), 60–61, 62, 63
Metropolitan Transit Authority, 64
Mexican-American population, 14, 103
Mexico, 8, 101–102
"Miami Nice" campaign, 66
Middle East, 24–25
Middle Eastern oil fields, 24
Migrant labor system, 104
Migration, 10; out of black areas, 73
Minorities, 4, 23, 52–53, 70, 131; voting strength of, 47
Minority Business Development Agency, 86

Minority power, 32
Mobil, 19
Model Cities, 18, 48–49, 50
Motor fuel, 12
Multinational firms, 70
Municipal garbage, 76
Municipal Utility Districts (MUDs), 7, 30, 35–36

National Aeronautic and Space Administration (NASA), 18, 22, 57
Neighborhood: amenities, 77, 90; change, 55; conflict, 56; groups, 55; maintenance, 68; organizations, 60–63; revitalization, 78; stabilization, 58–59, 78
Neighborhoods, 75–78; minority, 47
New Orleans, LA., 5, 11, 15
New York, 13, 19, 23, 27
Newsweek, 3
North Sea, 24

Office: buildings, 19–20; facilities, 14; towers, 21
Oil, 12–13; capital, 7; center, 11–14; company, 19; equipment companies, 13; fields, 14–15; prices, 4, 24–26; production, 13; service companies, 13; tools, 18
Oil industry, 7–8, 12, 19, 25, 57; and growth, 9; competition in, 16; concentration, 12–14, 19; federal investment in, 17–18
Oklahoma, 15
Oligopoly capitalism, 12–14
OPEC, 24

Paginas Amarillas, 120
Parks, 59–60
Pasadena, TX., 32, 63
Petrochemical: industry, 17, 21, 22–23, 57, 126–128; plants, 16–17, 20; research and development during World War II, 57
Petrochemicals, 16
Philadelphia, PA., 21, 38
Phillips, 19
Pittsburgh, PA., 16, 23, 27
Police, 40; protection, 62
Political: future, 134–136; power, 134–136; -power goals, 63
Population growth, 9; in incorporated areas, 32; in unincorporated areas, 32

Port Arthur, TX., 44
Port of Houston, 4, 15, 17, 25
Port of Houston Authority, 43
Poverty, 4; level, 86
Production class interests, 68–69
Pro-Houston, 65
Public housing, 46, 48, 80–82; projects, 45

Racial: discrimination, 73, 78, 79; homogeneity in neighborhoods, 58; integration, 59, 76; repression, 56; segregation, 59, 75
Racism, 74
Railroad: center, 5–6, 26; hub, 5; infrastructure, 11
Rayburn, Sam, 15
Real estate, 22; development, 17, 22; journals, 3; market, 3
Recession, oil, 9
Reconstruction Finance Corporation (RFC), 15–16
Redlining, 78
Regulatory era, 52
Regulatory Federalism, 50–52
Residential: neighborhoods, 75; neighborhoods in post–World War II growth spurt, 58
Reyes, Ben, 97
Reyes, Tina, 97
Rice, Mayor M. Baldwin, 43
Riceville (Houston), 76, 77
River Oaks (Houston), 67
Roads, 21
Rodriguez, Victoriano S., 102
Roosevelt, Franklin D., 15
Rosenberg, TX., 112

Sales workers, 14
San Antonio, TX., 14
San Francisco, CA., 5
Santa Fe Railroad, 103
Sassen-Koob, Saskia, 99
Saunders, Peter, 68
Sawmills, 76
School: children, 97; closing, 62; district, 34–35
Scott Street, 75
Segregation, 4, 73–74, 75–76
Selected advocacy era, 44–48, 52
Sewage discharge, 128–129
Shell, 19
"Shelly" decision, 58

Ship channel, 11
Shipping, 5
Smith v *Allwright*, 38
Smith Pipe Company, 87
Social: investment capital, 16; programs, 52; services, 18; welfare, 19
Socialism, 46
Southeast Houston, 75
Southern Pacific Railroad, 6, 11
Southwest Civic Club (SWCC), 59
Southwest Freeway, 47
Southwest sector, 76
Spring Branch (Houston), 81
Standard Oil, 13
Stauffer Chemical, 63
State-assisted oligopoly capitalism, 14–26, 41
State Department of Highways and Public Transportation, 65
State, intervention, 14, 16; subsidies, 11
State Highway Department, 64
Stofer, Patricia, 65
Suburban politics, 29
Suburbanization, 76
Sun Oil, 19
Sunbelt, 3, 27, 57; cities, 70

Tax subsidies, 18
Technology-distribution center, 24
Tejano families, 94
Territorial: control, 59–60; dominance, 30, 32
Texaco, 19
Texas Company, 11
Texas oil industry, 18–19
Texas Railroad Commission, 16
Texas Southern University, 74–75, 83
Third Ward (Houston), 61, 62, 71, 73, 78
Time, 3
Trade, international, 25

Traffic congestion, 64, 129–130
Transportation, 64; companies, 18

Underclass, 86
Undocumented: Central American immigrants, 98, 104–106; Hispanics, 100, 114–115, 116; Mexicans, 100; migrant workers, 103, 104; Salvadoran migrants, 98, 105–106
Unemployment, 70; rate, 4, 85
Unincorporated areas, 32
United States, 18
University of Houston, 74–75
Urban renewal, 23, 46, 55
U.S. Department of Justice, 38, 48
U.S. News and World Report, 3
U.S. Steel Chemical Co., 63

Vietnamese refugees, 82

War Production Board, 57
Wards, 78
Waste disposal facilities, 90–91
Water control and improvement districts (WCID), 35–36
Water districts, 35
Welch, Mayor Louis, 48–49, 50, 59
West Houston Association, 64–65
West University (Houston), 21
White-collar workers, 19, 20–21
White, Hattie Mae, 38
Whites, 78
Whitmire, Mayor, 53
Work force, 14
World oil economy, 23–24
World War I, 30
World War II, 9, 16–17, 18, 37

Zoning laws, 89; absence of, 23, 58